The Stor
RAF
Lulsgate Bottom

Ian James

REDCLIFFE
Bristol

First published by Redcliffe Press Ltd,
49 Park Street, Bristol BS1 5NT

ISBN 0 948265 48 5

Photoset and printed by WBC Print Ltd, Bristol

Contents

Acknowledgements

The author gratefully acknowledges the help of the following in compiling this account of RAF Lulsgate Bottom — Public Record Office (PRO); Ministry of Defence: Air Historical Branch (RAF), AR8b (RAF) and AR2b (RAF); Dept of Photographs, Imperial War Museum, London; Press/PRO. Avon and Somerset Constabulary; George Wimpey and Co. Ltd; Regimental Museum, The Gloucestershire Regiment; Dept. of the Air Force, 1361 St. Photo Squadron, Arlington, Virginia, USA. (B17 Photo No. 61858AC); Albert F. Simpson Historical Research Centre, Maxwell AFB, USA; M.D. Bills, *Air-Britain*; Kenneth S. West, (Photo: JU.88 at Lulsgate); Patricia Russell for Lulsgate plans; The many ex RAF staff, students, and others connected with RAF Lulsgate Bottom too numerous to mention with grateful thanks to all concerned; local farmers: M. J. Ashman, G. Ball, D. Marshall, E. V. Ogborne, A. G. Vauden, T. Williams; residents: Elsie Butt, Edith Cleeves, Rhona Rich, Alice Rogers, Mrs E. Hafner, Mrs R. Hurbert, Mrs L. Pearce and Mrs M. Taylor.

Bibliography

A Short History of the Royal Air Force Regiment, published by RAF Regiment Museum.

Attack Warning Red, D. Wood, published by MacDonald and Janes.

Impressments Log, Peter W. Moss, published by Air Britain.

Introduction

Many of those who pass through busy Bristol Airport alongside the A38 south of the city on their way to the sun, or use it on business, to learn to fly, or just go and watch the planes, may wonder at its early beginnings during World War Two. In those days, it helped train hundreds of pilots and instructors from the UK and Commonwealth, some of whom have returned as airline pilots in the years since the airfield was re-opened as Bristol's second airport in 1957, the original having been at Whitchurch.

This is the story of those far-off wartime days showing how the airfield quickly grew from a few acres to virtually the size it is today, and its effect on the local community.

Cornerpool Farm: where it all began.

1:   The search for a site

The first overtures towards an airfield at Lulsgate began on September 7th 1940, when 10 EFTS (Elementary Flying Training School) from 50 Group, Flying Training Command, under S/L T. W. Campbell AFC, moved into Weston-super-Mare with their Tiger Moths from Yatesbury in Wiltshire.

Soon after their arrival a search was made for a suitable site to establish a Relief Landing Ground (RLG) to ease the congestion and minimise damage to the airfield's surface during the winter months.

Eventually 14 acres of Cornerpool Farm run by H. Ogborne for J. Winstone of Belmont Farm, Wraxall, were initially acquired along the north side of the Bristol-Bridgwater road (A38) between Lulsgate and Redhill. The new RLG came into operation for dual training on September 28th, being cleared for solo flights from March 4th the following year. Incidentally, OC 'A' Flight at the time was F/L C. R. Cubitt, a pre-war Chief Pilot of Western Airways. Representative aircraft: R4752, R4758, and T7046, all Tiger Moth IIs.

The freezing winter of 1940/41 was the winter of the Blitz, and even country areas, especially those near large industrial centres such as Bristol, did not escape. At around 04.15 in the early hours of Monday, November 18th, a bomb hit the New Inn at Lulsgate. Hosts, Harry J. and Laura M. Sainsbury lost one of their two daughters, Molly Ellen (28) and her husband Gilbert Lovell (33). The Lovell's year-old baby Patricia, and Aunt, Mrs Emma Watkins, survived.

The Relief Landing Ground continued to be used by 10 EFTS, weather permitting, and its first recorded accident came on Saturday, February 15th, when Tiger Moth II, N9464, piloted by LAC A. E. Joyce, stalled from 30 feet on overshoot, hit the ground and overturned; fortunately Joyce was unhurt.

In March, Messrs. Northcote began constructing pill boxes and machine-gun posts.

During the night of Sunday/Monday, March 16th/17th 1941, Bristol's 5th Blitz raid, the Downside 'Starfish' decoy site to the west of the RLG on land belonging to the Fry's family was fired, along with others situated south west of Bristol. Attacked from 21.30 to 03.30, High Explosive bombs fell within a radius of $\frac{3}{4}$ mile, while incendiaries were strewn out to 2 miles; bombs that would otherwise have fallen on the city with obvious loss of human life. Cattle were killed and property damaged, including Goblin Combe Farm on the edge of the RLG. The farm, with its telephone, was used as a base for the RAF 'lighting' party. The Bristol decoys came within K10 Concealment and Deception Area, Col. Turner's Department, Air Ministry. HQ was originally at RAF Innsworth, Gloucester, under F/L (acting S/L from July 1942) D. C. Richardson, moving to Lulsgate on September 9th 1942. S/L R. A. Dimsdale took over the Area on January 12th 1944. The RAF personnel were billeted locally at Goblin Combe Farm, Warren House, and North Hill House, then off Downside Road. When Lulsgate opened personnel were housed on the camp.

Tiger Moth II, R5127, of 10 EFTS, crashed at Long Ashton on March 28th, unable to recover from a flat spin. The trainee pilot, LAC Villa, was seriously injured.

On the night of Thursday/Friday, April 3rd/4th, during a raid on Avonmouth, Goblin Combe was again affected, and the owners submitted a claim for compensation through the Air Ministry War Damage Department in Worcester Road, Bristol.

During Saturday, April 5th, the Downside 'Starfish' attracted a further large number of bombs. Two unexploded bombs landed on the edge of the RLG, as well as a number of incendiaries on the field itself. No one was hurt. The nearby village of Downside had a natural air-raid shelter not far away in the form of a large cave. Surprisingly, with the closeness of the 'Starfish', only one house was ever destroyed during the War; The Caves was owned by the Lock family, who were fortunately in the 'shelter' at the time, and the first they knew of it was when their dog, chain broken by the blast, came scurrying into the cave.

2: Beginnings

The month of May 1941 saw the start of transforming the RLG into an operational RAF station. The future development of Lulsgate had been considered towards the end of 1940, when a new home for the Fighter Experimental Unit at Middle Wallop was sought well away from possible invasion areas. Although the plan never materialised, construction went ahead, with provision for hard runways.

On Monday, May 26th, a Welshman, Mr Davis, took up his appointment as Air Ministry Resident Engineer for Lulsgate, and from Tuesday, June 10th, the RLG was no longer available to 10 EFTS.

Over the ensuing months further land was requisitioned, and farms affected included:

South and West of RLG
Goblin Combe   H. Ashman
Cornerpool   H. Ogborne for J. Winstone

North of RLG
Lulsgate   O. R. Vauden
Cook's   D. Marshall for H. Horler
Edson's }
Oatfield }   G. Ball
Downside   Mr Hart, believed to have been a Naval officer.
Stone   H. Flowers
Plus land from Mr V. Payne (?) and Kate Ball (George Ball's sister).

In at least one known case the farmer was not even allowed to harvest his fields, and as compensation received only the seed value. Stone Farm disappeared altogether, the farmhouse eventually becoming part of the new Station complex.

On a local note, Muriel, wife of Doug Marshall from Cook's Farm, taught at the local school situated alongside the A38, west of the entrance to Downside Road.

Construction of the airfield was entrusted, initially, to George Wimpey & Co. Ltd., as main contractor, and with the cutting of the first 'sod' on Wednesday, June 11th, the RLG ceased to exist. Mr

Patterson was Wimpey's Site Representative, and a physical fitness addict. Lulsgate was one of 93 wartime airfields for which Wimpey were responsible. Their Quantity Surveyor covering Lulsgate was C. E. Adams. T. W. Barrington was local AM Works Superintendent based at Langford Lodge, Pembroke Road, Bristol. Building began on June 26th, and work commenced on the main east/west runway on July 2nd. Sub-contractors, W. J. Pople & Sons of Burnham-on-Sea, started defence unit buildings on the 15th. Tons of hardcore were excavated from Goblin Combe Farm, helped by the stray German bomb!

Probably the new airfield's first visitor was most unexpected. Early on the morning of Thursday, July 24th 1941, residents of Weston and Clevedon were awakened by the sound of a low-flying aircraft with an unusual engine note. The weather was fine, and those who ventured to look may have seen the outline of a twin-engined bomber. After firing signal cartridges, it flew inland and at 06.20 a German Junkers Ju.88A-6, w/n 3457, coded 4D+DL of 3/KG30 'Adler' (Staffel letter 'D' in yellow) landed on what was to become Lulsgate's runway 21. The crew believed they had crossed the English and not the Bristol Channel after a raid on Birkenhead. They had apparently confused Beacon 173 near their base at Lanvéoc (Poulmic) by Brest with the Meacon decoy beacon at Lympsham near Weston-super-Mare operating on the same frequency, and in the early morning mist Avonmouth's balloon barrage probably looked very like that protecting Brest. The crew: Unteroffizier Wolfgang Hosie (pilot), Feldwebel Paul Zimmermann (observer), Obergefreiter Franz Sander (wireless operator), and Obergefreiter Robert Riemann (gunner), were all promptly 'arrested' by a very surprised mechanical digger driver, whose mate alerted the airfield's military guard provided by the King's Own Royal Regiment. Members of 10 EFTS flew over from Weston in their Tiger Moths to see the Junkers before it was flown by S/L H. J. Wilson to Farnborough with a Hurricane escort on August 1st for evaluation, appearing with RAF serial EE205, a fortnight later.

The airfield's military guard were housed in tents alongside the A38 adjacent to the main entrance of the present airport. Their spartan existence contrasted with the relative comfort of Wimpey's wooden section-hutted living site and offices nearby, which included the AM Resident Engineer's office. The army were soon provided with improved hutted accommodation including messing facilities with a separate one for officers.

Towards the end of 1941, Nelson R. Russell replaced Mr Davis as AM Clerk of Works.

P/O M. O. Robinson arrived at Colerne on November 10th from Middle Wallop to co-ordinate the distribution of stores and equipment for Lulsgate which had been arriving since August, eventually moving to the new airfield himself on December 4th.

On December 6th, a Spitfire IIa of 417 Squadron from Charmy Down near Bath, landed for information and damaged a wing.

There is an unsubstantiated report that Wimpey workers were taken on joy flights.

By the end of 1941, work was in hand on the Communal and Living Sites off Backwell Hill Road to the north of the airfield. On the airfield itself the Main Site and HQ around Stone Farm (now the airport's cargo area) were also under construction. Cable laying by G.E.C. had begun on November 14th.

Stone Farm today.

Turning into Downside Road from the A38 by the New Inn (now The Airport Tavern) today, you will pass a short distance down on the lefthand side the bases for one of the barrack blocks and those of

10

contractors' huts. Further along on the same side the gymnasium still stands. It was also used as a chapel and cinema. Dances, boxing matches, and other entertainments, including plays and Christmas pantomimes, were held there. The gym was probably completed during the airfield's expansion under Flying Training Command by Wimpey's successor, Trollop & Coles, in 1943. One of the new contractor's site foremen was Mr Wellings. Other facilities nearby included an educational block and the sports equipment store (which also survives). The turning into Backwell Hill Road lies opposite the gym, and a little way up on the right stands a small council estate where the Communal Site was situated on ground, known as The Drove, acquired from Lulsgate Farm. Some of the original buildings remain. This site was the key to the comfort and welfare of the Station and included messes for officers, NCOs, airmen, and later WAAFs.

Further up the hill on the left were the WAAF's barracks consisting of 'seco' huts built by Trollop & Coles in 1943. The site, which included a laundry and hairdressing shop, was constructed on George Ball's land near Oatfield Farm. After the War it was used by displaced persons such as Poles and Lithuanians.

The road bends around to the left at this point, and on the opposite corner lies the white edifice of Oatfield Cottage, originally known as Journey's End when built by Milton Bros. for B. Cleeves, a retired policeman, who also at one time worked for Wimpey on the airfield. Just past it is a steep entrance to the right leading to a lane climbing to Oatfield Wood, where Living Sites 2 and 3 were erected for officers and airmen on land from Downside Farm. It is believed use was also made of land belonging to Kate Ball.

Although probably not appreciated fully in wartime, the view from here is magnificent: to the south one looks down on Bristol Airport already 592 feet above sea level, before taking in the Mendip Hills beyond. To the west lies the Bristol Channel with Steep and Flat Holms visible on a fine day. Finally, to the north, Bristol, the Brecon Hills, and the Cotswold escarpment stretching away to the south-east towards Bath.

The main mode of transport was, inevitably, the bicycle, but during the winter toboggans may have been more appropriate!

On the left of Backwell Hill Road is the entrance to Oatfield Farm, followed by the ornate gates leading to Clappers, a large country house in its own grounds. This was requisitioned from a Major Wills of the tobacco family, being used by some Flying Training Command COs. It had no electricity, so a motor-driven generator was used to provide power. The water supply came from a well in the grounds. After the War it became the home of helicopter pioneer, Raoul

'Winstones' — station sick quarters — today.

Hafner. From Clappers the road bears around to the right, where Living Site 1 housed the sergeants' quarters. All three living sites comprised of Nissen huts.

Opposite the Communal Site a stand-by generator and coal compound were situated on land belonging to W. T. Crane of Old Farm, near a gypsy encampment which the RAF tried unsuccessfully to move. The generator was maintained in a readiness state around the clock by the Cleeves brothers, Thomas, George and Robert. The latter ran his own garage at Downside with the help of his wife Edith, and when it was available provided petrol for RAF personnel lucky enough to have the use of a motor-car or motor-bike. Others may have utilised the car hire service run by Elsie Butt of Flax Bourton.

Past the Cleeves' garage, set back a little from the road on the right, stands Winstones. This large detached house, built by Child Bros. in the 'thirties, was eventually requisitioned from Mrs F. W. Mackeson for use as the Station Sick Quarters, and a temporary 'seco' extension was put up in the grounds.

A small sewage plant serving the Station was situated on Mr Ball's land on the opposite side of the Downside Road to Cook's Farm.

A High Frequency Transmitting Station constructed on land owned by Mr T. Williams of Felton House Farm, Felton was manned by three airmen.

On the airfield, the Main Site was the technical and administrative heart of the Station. Six double fighter pens plus air raid shelters were built beside the peritrack along the southern and eastern boundaries. In addition, three circular 20 feet diameter hardstandings were provided. Three 69 feet double and four single blister hangars, plus one Bellman were erected (the Bellman is still in use). This included two single blisters alongside the A38 put up when the airfield was an RLG.

The Bellman hangar was introduced in 1938 as a standard light transportable unit, many being replaced early in the War by the larger 'T2' designed by the Tees-Side Bridge and Engineering Company. Nissen huts were the invention of a Canadian mining engineer of the Great War, L/Col P. Nissen DSO.

Three tarmac runways forming the usual triangular pattern were constructed under the standard Air Ministry specification of 2" ashes, 9" hardcore, and 3" tarmacadam. They were originally known by numbers 1 to 6 in a clockwise direction from north, then from March 5th 1944 by their QDM's (magnetic headings) rounded up or down to the nearest whole number (275 would be rounded up to 280) and indicated by the first two digits: 2/5 became 28/10: 3891 feet × 150 feet; 1/4 became 21/03: 3300 feet × 150 feet; and 3/6 became 34/16: 3294 feet × 150 feet.

The airfield had five Dispersals, numbers 1 to 5 used also at one time by army defence personnel for sleeping. Near Dispersal 3 on the opposite side of Cook's Bridal Path which formed the airfield's western boundary, stood Warren House situated to the south of the Downside 'Starfish'. It was brought by Mr F. Burgess from Mrs K. Gibson, a widow, who had a smaller property built at Willis's Batch. East of the Decoy was North Hill House owned by the Fry's, and to the north, Downside House Farm, residence of Dr A. Jowett BSC.

There were three entrances leading to the airfield. From the A38 near the contractors' huts, from Downside Road to Stone Farm, and from Cook's Bridal Path in to Dispersal 2. Other temporary ones existed for the benefit of contractors.

Gun testing butts were laid out near the southern boundary.

Later in the War, Dispersal 5 on Cornerpool Farm was used to house Italian prisoners-of-war. They became well known in the area, and one of the characters to emerge was a gentleman named Scarparelli (?). Somerset had a number of POW camps: Wookey Hole, Goathurst near Bridgwater and Colley Lane, Bridgwater, Wells, Barwick near Yeovil, Norton Fitzwarren and Brockley. The local Pioneer Corps Group HQ administering the camps was at Norton Fitzwarren, Taunton. In Gloucestershire the Group HQ was at Miserden House, Miserden, with Base Camp at Blockley. Italians were accommodated at Ashton and Bedminster, Bristol, and Brockworth, Broadwell, Coleford, Churchdown, Patchway, and Yate. German camps were at Bourton-on-the-Hill, Cheltenham, and Winchcombe.

As will be seen, Lulsgate was far from complete when it opened at the beginning of 1942, construction continuing as the airfield expanded into 1944.

Further firms subcontracted during 1942/43 were Clark Bros. of Swindon and F. J. Burnett from Wrington as a maintenance engineer.

By now the War was receding from the West Country. Colerne near Bath succeeded Filton as Fighter Sector airfield on April 25th 1941. Filton transferred to 44 Group, Ferry Command, on December 8th the same year. A satellite for Colerne had already been established at Charmy Down during November 1940. Another fighter airfield in the area was therefore unnecessary and Lulsgate became relegated to the secondary role of anti-aircraft co-operation, before switching to the important task of flying training, with the added advantage of its hard runways, an unusual feature for such airfields at the time.

3: Arrivals

On Friday, January 2nd 1942, Spitfire IIA, P8071, of 417 Squadron, Charmy Down, piloted by Sgt D. C. Goudie, landed in the gathering dusk on an obstructed runway. No-one was hurt. Two days later, on Sunday, January 4th, S/L N. M. Corcos from 10 Group Fighter Command's HQ at Rudloe Manor near Bath became the Station's first Commander. S/L Corcos had been on operational duties with 10 Group's HQ since its inception during the early summer of 1940. Before the War he was a newspaper man, and during 1932/33 was temporary Morocco correspondent for *The Times*. On January 5th, F/L A. N. David was posted in from Middle Wallop as Station Adjutant. F/O H. Bainbridge arrived from Colerne to be in charge of transport on the 8th. P/O L. F. Smith from Manston, originally for Station defence duties, stayed 24 hours before moving to Tangmere: his place was taken two days later on the 12th by P/O P. S. Saundercock from Predannack.

On the 10th, as a prelude to the arrival of the airfield's first residents, S/L H. R. Allen DFC, ex CO of 66 Squadron, now CO of 286 (Anti-Aircraft Co-operation) Squadron, motto: 'We Exercise Our Defences', visited Lulsgate with his Flight Commander, F/L Thornton-Brown, and Adjutant, F/O Duveen.

A group of officers from 263 Squadron at Charmy Down visited the Station on the 14th.

From January 4th to 12th, officers and men slept on the Communal Site and fed with the Army alongside the A38. Conditions were crude and the cold intense. On the 12th the RAF messes opened without floor covering and few tables and chairs. Officers were able to get some hot water in their huts for early morning shaving, but many NCOs washed and shaved in cold water, preferring to break the ice rather than postpone their toilet until they arrived at the Communal Site. There was only cold water and inadequate lighting in the airmen's ablution block. Worse still, at the time water pipes had not been laid and water had to be fetched in buckets — of which there were only four at one stage. Neither was the sewage farm fully operational and the drains could not be used. Electricity, although laid to the three Living Sites, remained unconnected, while the toilets were chemical Elsans. The water supply terminated at the Communal

Site and it was some time before it reached to the Living Sites providing more comfortable conditions for ablutions and showers. Wimpey's had found the provision of water a problem during early construction work.

Other problems that presented themselves included the narrowness of the roads for vehicles to pass, difficulties in lining men up for parades and inspections, and the isolated bath units.

In a blizzard, RAF Lulsgate Bottom was officially declared 'operational' on Thursday, January 15th. It was originally to have been known as RAF Broadfield Down but the name was changed before opening. The following Sunday the first church parade was conducted by Cpt. H. Crane, padré with 'C' Company, 6th Battalion, KORR, still carrying out airfield defence duties with 120 men under Cpt. Anslow. The nearest places of worship outside the camp were St Katherine's, Felton, where the Revd. David Jones, MA was the incumbent, and a Methodist Chapel at Downside.

On the 19th, F/L H. T. Bird arrived from Hunsdon to take command of Station defence on behalf of the RAF. When his Ack-Ack Flight (it never received a number) arrived at Yatton Station direct from training at Cardington, they were unsure of the new airfield's location, and it was left to a local lad among them, AC2 R. Fox, to lead the march up Brockley Combe. Equipment was to consist of Brens, Stens, and mounted Lewis guns. A Battle HQ was established near the north taxiway.

During the first years of the War, light anti-aircraft (LAA) defence and security for airfields was not only entrusted to the Army, but the RAF trained their own ground gunners as well, and this led to problems in command decisions. Defences were strained during the crucial summer of 1940 and a document, the Taylor Report, was published suggesting a single organisation should be responsible for the task. The Air Ministry and War Office accepted the findings and went ahead with plans to develop an airfield defence force. At the beginning of 1941, the Army began providing the RAF with Local Defence Advisers, but the War Office were unable to meet their defence responsibilities in full, and the RAF Regiment was born on January 6th 1942. Despite the presence of the Ack-Ack Flight, the Army continued in the airfield defence role at Lulsgate. The LDA allocated to the Station was L/Col C. L. Weymiss.

Other officers and NCOs had started to arrive:

W/O S. J. Vought	Signals	from Biggin Hill	on the 15th
Sgt W. H. Warburton	Armourer	" 93 Sqn	" " 16th
F/L D. O. Bowes	Medical Officer	" 79 Sqn	" " 17th
F/L B. M. Hatfield	Accounts Officer	" Castle Camps	" " 17th

P/O R. J. Alderson	Engineering	" Middle Wallop "	" 20th
W/O W. G. Holder	Disciplinarian	" Ouston	" " 27th

On Saturday, January 24th, part of 286 Squadron under S/L Allen arrived from Filton, aircraft being positioned on hardstandings alongside the A38 and near Dispersal 5, the rest of the Squadron being located at various airfields in the area as requirement demanded. Besides S/L Allen members included:

Officers:
F/Ls Thornton-Brown, Burrows and Boddington
F/O Rawlins
P/Os Sherman, Hill, Duveen and Ames

NCO Flying Personnel:
Pilots:
F/Sgt Nicholls
Sgts Diggins and Lister
W/Op/Air Gunners:
F/Sgts Gouldson, Hunt, Jennings, Spence and White
Sgts Dove, Hogan, O'Reilly and Roy
Plus 210 airmen

While at Lulsgate, 'Dizzy' Allen was to meet and marry Anne, daughter of G/C R. Smyth-Pigott from nearby Brockley Hall. The Hall was requisitioned by the military and housed American troops, the Smyth-Pigott family having to move into Brockley Cottage. After the War, the Hall was sold to the local council and converted into flats.

Like a number of wartime COs, Dizzy had a dog, a white bull terrier called Crippen which he exercised by riding his bike around the airfield while the dog trotted behind. He also owned a cocker spaniel named Pookie.

286 Squadron had been formed originally as 10 Group AAC Unit in 1941, becoming 286 Squadron on November 17th that year. Equipment consisted of Oxfords, Masters, and Hurricanes. Duties involved flying pre-arranged courses to provide targets for the searchlights and range finders of local anti-aircraft batteries.

Two days after their arrival, 286 were joined by No. 3 Detachment from 116 (Calibration) Squadron who moved over from Colerne. It consisted of six men under F/L T. W. Burrows, their equipment being three 15cwt Fordson Wireless Tenders and their respective operators: EH 858 (Cpl Gregory), RMX 49 (F/L Burrows and Sgt Miles), and RMG 729 (F/Sgt Bradley).

At the beginning of 1942, 116 Squadron, motto: 'Precision in Defence', was based at Hendon under S/L E. D. Grundall with Lysanders and Hurricanes, their job being to carry out radar alignment and predictor checks for anti-aircraft units. Representative aircraft: Lysander III, Tl703, and Hurricane I, AG205. Originally, it had been formed from 1 Ack-Ack Calibration Flight at Hatfield on February 17th 1941, then equipped with Lysanders, moving to Hendon the following April. Detachments were dispersed to various parts of the country wherever their services were required.

Lulsgate's first administration and management team was divided into sections under the following officers and NCOs:

Officer Commanding:	S/L N. M. Corcos
Adjutant and Orderly Room:	F/L A. N. David
Engineering:	P/O R. J. Alderson
Equipment:	F/O M. O. Robinson
Accounts:	F/L B. M. Hatfield
Defence:	F/L H. T. Bird
Medical:	F/L D. O. Bowes
Signals:	W/O S. J. Vought
Armaments:	Sgt W. H. Warbourton
Disciplinarian:	W/O W. G. Holder
Watch Office:	Duty Pilots on rota from 286 Squadron
Transport:	F/O H. Bainbridge

Although supposedly operational, Lulsgate was nowhere near ready to receive residents. There was no control tower, only the Duty Pilot's hut on a temporary structure by the Fire Section. Flying aids were non-existent, and there was no proper airfield lighting. S/L Allen and F/L Thornton-Brown were billeted with other officers at Barley Wood House, Wrington, owned by Cpt Douglas Wills (retd.) of the tobacco family. However, the rest of the personnel had to rough it in the muddy morass, some airmen even sleeping on tables in the cookhouse until their billets were ready. Bedding was damp and, with coke in short supply, the men burnt anything they could lay their hands on in the Nissen hut stoves to dry out.

Off duty, when weather conditions would allow, some found their way to local hostelries where a warmer welcome awaited them, while others had passes to Bristol.

During the War a number of public houses in the area became favourite haunts, and the following are a few examples with their respective hosts:

The Bridge	Yatton	Mr and Mrs Baker (?)
The Bungalow	Butcombe	Mrs Edith Rogers and daughter-in-law, Alice
The Churchill Inn	Churchill	Mr and Mrs Gittins
The Crown	Ridgehill	Vernon Patch (originally an off-licence)
The Darlington Arms	Redhill	Eric House

The Fox and Goose	Barrow Gurney	Harry and Edith Patch
The George	Backwell	Bert Brown
The George and Dragon	Felton	Jack and Lou Franks
The Golden Lion	Wrington	Mrs 'Daisy' Priddy
The Jubilee	Flax Bourton	Fred and Maude Marguerite
The Mill Inn	Butcombe	George and Elsie Lambert
The New Inn	Backwell	Mr and Mrs Harry Miller
The New Inn	Lulsgate	Harry and Laura Sainsbury
The Plough	Wrington	Mr and Mrs Richard Fowler
The Rising Sun	Backwell	Bill and Christine Coggins
The Star	Rhodyate Hill	Mr and Mrs Harry Garton
The Waggon and Horses	Potters Hill	Mr and Mrs Bill Ward

In Bristol there was the officers' bar in The Mauretania at the bottom of Park Street run by Avery's, and the W. D. & H. O. Wills social hall.

The feelings and memories of all their wartime customers are summed up in the following poem, written after the War by Cpl C. C. Sharp of the RASC while stationed at Freetown, West Africa, in 1946:

Good Days

It's a long long way from this place
an inn that I used to know.
There's miles of ocean 'tween me
and an inn called 'The Bungalow'.

There'd gather there of an evening
in the flickering shadowed light,
a company who'd tarry awhile
as gathered the Winter night.

The darts flew, the skittles shook,
fast and merry the fun,
and the people who met will never forget
the beer that was second to none.

We'd talk of the battles of Europe
and plan the campaigns far ahead,
and when they turned out quite different,
we'd smugly say, "Just as we said".

Someone may state an opinion
that black skies would soon become blue,
and triumphantly go on to add
that Churchill agreed with him too.

And thus for a time we'd recapture
a breath of the former life,
and forget ours of the present
was seething with hatred and strife.

And when the revels were over,
and we stepped out into the rain,
the evening air was pleasant to smell
and earth seemed good again.

Some pedalled home on their cycles,
while others drove off in cars.
There were those who cared for neither,
and walked home under the stars.

But now it's all very rusty,
and it all seems a long time ago,
that we all laughed and chatted together
at an inn called 'The Bungalow'.

Not far from The Bungalow is Butcombe Court. It is believed at one time to have been a rest centre for the Green Howards, and it became the temporary home of Clifton College's Preparatory School when they were evacuated from Bristol, while the Senior School moved to Cornwall, re-opening at Bude on February 11th 1941.

During March/April 1941, plans to re-organise and extend Bristol's anti-aircraft defences were introduced. The number of

The Bungalow Inn, Butcombe (photograph: Alice Rogers).

permanent sites would be increased from thirteen to twenty, Site 20 being established on Backwell Hill. Four 3.7″ Mobiles with ½352 Bty, 112th HAA Regiment, became its first occupants when they moved in from Failand (Site 16A) during May 6th/7th. Gun Laying radar arrived later. The rest of the Battery with their remaining four 3.7″ Mobiles positioned at Pagan's Hill, Chew Stoke (Site 18), on the 10th, from Ashton Park (Site 15A).

During the War, John Lysaght's, the Bristol engineering firm, built Crusader tanks using a testing ground at the top of Backwell Hill which included a large water pit.

A Hurricane II BD941 from 87 Squadron, Charmy Down, crashed at Naish Farm, Clapton-in-Gordano, on February 8th. The RCAF pilot, Sgt J. R. Keith, was killed.

Returning to Lulsgate, the NAAFI opened on February 10th 1942, but only at certain times and with strict rationing.

On the 17th, F/O Bainbridge was detailed to lead a Station Fire Committee.

Because of the obvious shambles, and with the HQ complex still incomplete, plans were made to move 286 Squadron to Colerne until the Station was in a fit state to receive it.

The AOC 10 Group, Air Commodore A. H. Orlebar CBE AFC (he had replaced AVM Sir C. J. Quintin Brand KBE DSO MC DFC on July 22nd, 1941) carried out a personal inspection on March 1st. The 116 Squ Detachment left for Hendon on the same day, and final members of 286 departed for Colerne the day after.

March 16th saw 'C' Company, KORR, leave for St Just in Cornwall, to be replaced the next day by 'B' Company, 70th (Young Soldiers) Battalion, Gloster Regiment, with 120 men under Cpt E. A. Toms. Battalion HQ was at Burnham-on-Sea, but moved to Glastonbury in June. The Company initially had their meals on the Communal Site until their own mess was ready on the airfield.

On April 26th, 46th AA Brigade who covered Bristol's AA defences under orders from 8th AA Division, carried out a light anti-aircraft recce of Lulsgate.

From June 1st, F/L Bird was based at South Cerney but on detachment to Lulsgate for RAF Regiment duties. He was on a Regimental course at Brampton during the month, eventually leaving the Service in January 1943.

The Army finally gave up defence duties on August 5th 1942, when the Glosters left for Ilfracombe, but not before they had been called to assist the local authorities in the aftermath of the two 'Baedeker' raids on Weston-super-Mare, June 28th/29th. The Devonshire's 12th Battalion relieved them at Lulsgate for the duration from July 1st to 5th.

L/Col Weymiss left on November 12th 1942, to be replaced as LDA by a Major Black. P/O Leafe of the RAF Regiment arrived from Hullavington to take up Defence Officer duties on December 3rd. Members of the Ack-Ack Flight were posted to North Africa, to be absorbed into a squadron of the new regiment. The original 150 unnumbered RAF defence squadrons formed during April 1941 were numbered 701 to 850 inclusive on December 19th 1941, acquiring the prefix '2' from February 1st 1942. Uniforms at the time were khaki battledress.

Before leaving the Army one must not forget that much-maligned force, the Home Guard. Two Somerset Battalions covering the local area were the 7th (Long Ashton) and in addition 13th (Axbridge) from May 1943. One company was based at Wrington among whose members were Cpts Anson and Bell as well as a Sgt Owen. A platoon situated at Downside was under Sgt Charlie Lock, along with Cpl (later Sgt) Eddie Briffett, while another at Redhill was commanded by 2nd/Lt Titman. Although Sgt Lock was senior man at Downside, orders came via Eddie Briffett as he had a telephone in his house, Highfields in Winters Lane, Wrington. The Home Guard were originally known as Local Defence Volunteers, but the title was changed during July 1940 on instructions from Winston Churchill.

Construction work and organisation of the aerodrome continued apace. An AM engineer at Lulsgate during 1942/43 was J. R. Donaldson.

On March 21st, 1942 the PBX became operational, and the Orderly Room ceased to be used as a telephone exchange.

A Spitfire Vb AD553 of 312 Squadron from Fairwood Common, crashed near Axbridge Station on April 27th killing the Czech pilot, F/L Rohacek.

With the completion of the Station HQ, 286 Squadron returned on April 30th under their new CO, M. C. B. Boddington DFC, now promoted to S/L. As before their aircraft, which now included Defiants, were dispersed to various airfields in 10 Group for AAC duties: Colerne (Oxford/Defiant); Middle Wallop and Rhoose (Defiant); Exeter, Carew Cheriton, Perranporth, and Harrowbeer (Master); Fairwood Common (Oxford); and Kemble (Hurricane). No more than one or two aircraft were based at each Station at any one time. Aircraft examples: Defiant I, V1115; Oxford I, DF254; Master IIIs, W8837 and W8851; Hurricane I, V7540. Code letters were NW. 286 Squadron finally moved to Zeals on May 26th, and Lulsgate transferred from Fighter Command to 23 Group, Flying Training Command, on June 1st, 1942.

4: Satellite to South Cerney

From June 1st, Lulsgate became one of two satellites for the South Cerney based 3(P)AFU, (Pilot) Advanced Flying Unit, with Oxford Is and IIs, the other being Long Newnton near Tetbury. Aircraft were fitted with TR9 radios and major maintenance was carried out at South Cerney.

There was strong support at one time to transfer 3 OTU (Operational Training Unit) from Cranwell, but it eventually moved to Haverford West and Templeton in West Wales.

3(P)AFU's CO was G/C N. Carter DFC, CFI was W/C C. F. Macpherson until October 11th, followed by W/C D. S. Radford from the 22nd. The CFI and Detachment Commander at Lulsgate was S/L B. E. Moody AFC who took up his appointment from June 12th. S/L Corcos left Lulsgate on September 24th, taking up a new post with 3(P)AFU at South Cerney the following day.

Normally there would have been no Station CO as such while the airfield was being used as a satellite; technically the post would have been held by the parent unit CO. S/L Moody, although he is known to have lived in the officer's mess, may have used 'Clappers' at some time.

The Detachment had three Flights, two day: 'A' and 'B', and a Night Flight. During August, Deputy CFI at Lulsgate was F/L G. B. Gillie, 'A' Flight Commander: F/L G. K. Woollard, with F/L A. E. Palmer, OC 'B' Flight. Other instructors included F/Os M. G. T. Allen and R. O. Whitehead.

(Pilot) Advanced Flying Units were formed to familiarise Empire trained pilots from various foreign and Commonwealth countries as well as the UK with our operational practices and conditions, and in some cases the language!

Prior to March 1942, 3(P)AFU was known as 3 SFTS (Service Flying Training School).

On June 20th F/L D.O. Bowes, the MO, was posted to 9 AFU at Hullavington, and based there until going to India in July 1943.

Lulsgate aircraft made use of other local airfields for circuits and landings such as Yate, Whitchurch, and Weston Zoyland.

The three Flights were dispersed to the south of the main runway.

In 1943 there was a change in Flight letters: 'A' became 'J', and the Night Flight, 'Z'.

F/L Woollard continued as OC 'J' Flight, but in September 1943 was probably OC 'Z' Flight, which included the following pilots:

P/Os: Burge, Davis, and Knight.   F/Sgts: Shorney and Bolter.
F/Os: Clark and Yates.   Sgt: Fisher.

S/L H. F. R. Bradbury was at Lulsgate from August 24th to September 28th and CI 'C' Squadron F/O Whitehead moved to 7 Flying Instructors School (FIS), Upavon, on August 30th. F/O K. J. Hardman arrived during June 1942 as Electrical and Instruments Officer until he was posted on June 27th the following year. Just before leaving he was appointed Station Fire Officer and sent on a two-week course to Sutton-on-Hull. The airfield fire tender was in the care of a Cpl Harper. During this period there were over 100 u/t Wireless Operators/Air Gunners at Lulsgate awaiting posting.

With the planned expansion of Lulsgate as a training airfield with its own lodger units, WAAFs were to be posted in, and at a meeting on August 15th 1942 it was decided to use Winford Manor, owned by the Cripps family (Sir Stafford), as temporary quarters until their permanent site in Backwell Hill Road was completed. It is possible that Winford Manor may have been used at one time by male officers, as well as WAAFs. Earlier, in May, S. J. Clark remembers being posted to Lulsgate as a Wireless Mechanic fresh from his course at Cranwell, and promptly being put on fire-watching duties there.

The large increase in training movements led inevitably to accidents. Some were minor such as that to Oxford I, BG599, at Weston Zoyland on August 2nd, 1942 when no-one was hurt. But others proved fatal: on September 22nd at 05.20 Oxford I, W6610, dived into the ground from a considerable height for reasons undetermined, killing the two Australians on board, P/O N. L. Casely and Sgt J. N. Harvey. Two Fleet Air Arm Fairey Fulmar Is collided in mid-air over the airfield on October 15th, one pilot, Sub/Lt Shorte in N4079 died of multiple injuries, the other, Sub/Lt Starkey flying N4008 bailed out unhurt, but was detained in the Station Sick Quarters overnight. The aircraft were from 761 Squadron, Yeovilton.

3(P)AFU ceased using Lulsgate for a brief period during late October and early November 1942, probably due to wet weather producing low cloud and poor visibility making flying training impossible. Something Lulsgate has continued to suffer with to the present day.

Interesting aircraft used by the Unit for communications during the summer of '42 were three impressed civil machines: DH80A Puss Moth, BM995 (ex.G-ABLP); DH87B Hornet Moth, W9387 (ex.G-ADIR); and DH94 Moth Minor, W6458 (ex.G-AFPC).

Pearl Harbour on December 7th 1941 had officially precipitated the USA into the War, and in the European Theatre they decided to make Bristol and its port of Avonmouth a main entry point by sea for supplies to the UK.

Bristolians soon became used to this friendly 'occupation' of the city, but that is another story. An area of Filton airfield, still known to locals as the American Site, was used for assembling aircraft delivered by sea from the States as well as repair. It become IX Base Aircraft Assembly Depot, part of the 9th Air Force's IX Air Service Command, and Filton was given the Station Number 803. When HQ United States Strategic Air Forces, Europe, was set up to administer the 8th, 9th, and 15th Air Forces in May 1944 Filton came under Air Service Command USSTAF.

During 1942, a camp housing mainly negro engineers was constructed on the north-side of the A370, Bristol to Weston-super-Mare road, at Brockley.

A number of military hospitals were developed by the Americans in the Bristol area including: 74th US General Hospital established in grounds owned by the Wraxall family at Tyntesfield; Frenchay, which at one time housed the 298th and 117th US Hospitals; and another on Lord Ducie's estate at Tortworth, Gloucestershire, under the 53rd US Medical Service during May 1943 is known to have housed the 91st and 120th US Hospitals. Around the end of the War it is reported POWs were held at Tortworth. After the end of hostilities Tyntesfield disbanded, the camp at Brockley being used for a time by Long Ashton RDC to house displaced War families. Frenchay was handed over for civil use, while Tortworth eventually became HM Prison Leyhill.

After its evacuation, Clifton College is believed to have been used by the Royal Army Service Corps, and as 'D' Day approached became the HQ of American General Omar H. Bradley, who commanded the US 1st Army under Montgomery's 21st Army Group. It included General Leonard T. Gerow's V Corps which, along with its 1st Infantry Division, was to suffer badly in the debacle of Omaha beach, east of the Vire River, on June 6th, 1944.

USAAC Piper L4 Cub communication aircraft are known to have used a field off Beggars Bush Lane, west of the Suspension Bridge.

Down at Brockley Combe a rest centre for American convoys was established prior to 'D' Day.

5:   Crash landing

The first month of 1943 brought tragic excitement to Lulsgate. On January 23rd at 16.00, Boeing B.17F Fortress, 41-24579, coded 'PU-F', and named after the Walt Disney character Thumper the rabbit, crash-landed alongside runway '2', ending up close to the western boundary near Goblin Combe Farm. It belonged to 360 Squadron, 303rd Bomber Group, US 8th Air Force, based at Molesworth, Huntingdonshire, and was returning badly damaged from a raid on Lorient.

Thumper had originally taken off from Molesworth at 10.46 to join a force briefed to attack the submarine pens at Lorient, with Brest as a secondary target. Approaching Lorient the B.17 was attacked by Focke-Wulf Fw.190s causing the premature release of three bombs. The aircraft continued to its target and dropped the remaining bombs from 23,000 feet at approximately 13.45. Under continual harrassment from fighters and flak, part of the plexiglass in the nose was torn away leaving the navigator and bombardier facing a freezing gale. A shell burst in the cockpit badly damaging the instrument panel, rendering the hydraulics useless, and starting a small fire which the captain, 1st/Lt J. A. Castle, managed to put out. Control cables were hit, maps and radio destroyed, navigation being reduced to dead-reckoning. No. 4 engine stopped, and No. 3 began vibrating so badly it threatened to break away from its mountings.

Clear of flak, Castle brought the crippled B.17 down low to shake off the fighters eager for the kill. Both turrets were out of action, and it was a relieved crew who watched the enemy turn for home as the English coast approached. Miraculously, the only serious injury was a bullet wound sustained by radio operator, T/Sgt E. J. Yannie.

Once over England it was obvious the aircraft would not reach Molesworth in the failing light, and a landing ground had to be found quickly. By the time Lulsgate came into view Thumper was flying very low and losing height all the time. It was decided that the two pilots (the other being 2nd/Lt K. M. Fitzsimmons, seconded from 427BS, 360BG) would stay with the aircraft and attempt a belly landing. The rest of the crew baled out. Sadly, all except Sgt Loll (photographer), suffered injuries in the process due to insufficient height for parachute deployment: 2nd/Lts C. L. Herman (navigator)

Boeing B17F 41-124579 'Thumper' (photograph: USAAF 61858AC).

and L. B. Sinopli (bombardier), S/Sgts M. Semonick and J. S. Klasnick (waist-gunners) were all treated at Lulsgate's Sick Quarters. T/Sgt M. Levin (engineer) and S/Sgt C. E. Craft (assistant radio operator) went to the Royal Naval Hospital at Barrow Gurney, along with T/Sgt Yannie who had broken legs in addition to his bullet wound. S/Sgt Staner (assistant engineer) jumped too low and his body was removed to Lulsgate.

The wheels-up landing was successful. It was fortuitous that there was no fire — the Station fire engine, in eagerness, drove a short-cut across the grass and became stuck in the mud. First on the scene were a member of the Home Guard, deployed the other side of the wall from where the B.17 ended up, and the Clerk of Works, Nelson Russell, in the AMWD van accompanied by the Equipment Officer, now F/O Blake.

A number of local people witnessed the crash, including a Mr Gibbs who, while hedging nearby with his wife, saw Yannie land and break his legs. Mr Gibbs thought a German raider had been shot down until he reached the injured American. Mrs R. Hurbert, staying with her husband at Cornwell Farm, tended another who broke his left ankle.

A day or so later a second Fortress arrived to take those crew members who could travel back to Molesworth. Sgts Yannie, Craft, and Levin were transferred to the 298th US Military Hospital at Frenchay; Craft on February 16th and the remaining two on April 13th.

As for Thumper, it was to be her last flight. She was removed by road under US Air Service Command supervision, and broken-up for salvage on January 30th.

When 3(P)AFU arrived at Lulsgate, a mobile flare-path was available for night flying: it being the duty of electricians and a W/Mech to lay it each night and remove it the next morning. The cables and lamps were paid out behind a lorry, the angle of approach indicators (AAIs) set up, and goosenecks positioned at the top end of the runway. If the wind changed during flying the whole lot had to be taken up and relaid. A mobile Chance light was situated at the junction of two runways, connected by landline to a telephone in the Flight Commander's hut which was near the main road. During the miseries of winter the duty W/Mech used to sit on the body of the Chance light with his back to the generator's radiator to keep warm.

A standard brick-built Control Tower was constructed in 1942 on the opposite side of the north taxiway to the earlier Watch Office/Duty Pilot's hut by the Fire Station. Communication was by HF and later VHF radio. The usual Aldis lamps and Verey pistols were available, and a signals square laid out near the new Tower, with airfield code letters 'LP' alongside in white.

Permanent runway and approach lighting was eventually installed in the form of the Drem Mk.II system, and is believed to have served all runways. Taxiway and obstruction lights were also provided. The civilian Air Ministry Works Department were responsible for airfield lighting maintenance. South-west of the airfield a red identification beacon flashed 'LP' in morse. By early 1945 as an addition to facilitate landing in poor visibility by day or night, sodium lights were installed.

The outer circle of Drem lights was situated on various farmers' land, including Broadfield House Farm (R. G. Bendall) to the south-west of Lulsgate.

By early 1944, Direction Finding equipment (D/F) for use in low or high power had been installed. The manual HF/DF Homer was situated to the east of the A38 opposite the airfield on land owned by Don Lovell of Collisters Brook Farm. A Mrs Gibbs lived nearby and used to supply D/F operators, among them Sgts Price, Saker and Wilson, with local provisions.

The RAF by now had established a separate flying control trade and an early Senior Flying Control Officer was F/O (later F/L) George Adams, assisted by F/Os Hall and (possibly) Green, both of whom were eventually promoted. During 1944, F/L A. E. Tattersall took over the ATC team as Senior Controller. A Meteorological Office was also opened in the Tower.

On March 12th, 1943, G/C F. H. Woolliams from 56 OTU became CO of 3(P)AFU in place of G/C North Carter who was posted to Bomber Command HQ. He visited Lulsgate on April 1st to discuss the proposed formation there of 1540 BATF (Beam Approach Training Flight). Four days later F/L G. Lambert was made CO (elect), and the first of eight modified Oxford Is were collected from

South Cerney on the 20th. Others followed at intervals and the last two were delivered on May 6th, the same day as the new Standard Beam Approach (SBA) was flight tested. The SBA building was situated under the approach to runway 5 on land acquired from Goblin Combe Farm known as Tom Tuff field. The equipment had a front beam 1.9° wide with a range of 45 miles, and a back beam 2° wide — range, 50 miles. The inner and outer markers on the approach to runway 2 gave a satisfactory reception at the 3000 feet test height. These were on land belonging to Down House Farm, Felton, (C. Rendall) and Court Farm, Winford, (H. Cole), respectively. On April 24th a working party arrived to install the Link Trainer but found the room was not quite ready.

F/L Lambert was not, after all, made CO but joined 1513 BATF at Bramcote in Warwickshire. S/L J. A. Gordon AFC was confirmed in the post on May 10th. The next day F/O W. E. Wesson became one of the first instructors (BATFs did not have CFIs), and No. 1 Course began on May 26th, although the flight offices were not completed until June 7th.

The Unit's first eight aircraft were (with their known individual letters): V4224/J, V4223/K, LB450/M, MP401/N, LB454/P, LB451/Q, DF259/S and MP294 (letter unknown) which returned to South Cerney for modifications on May 14th.

All aircraft were in standard trainer camouflage of dark green/dark earth top surfaces and yellow undersides, as were those of 3(P)AFU and 10 EFTS before them, but they carried an additional yellow triangle on the nose denoting their SBA status which included the aircraft letter in black.

The Flight's HQ with its offices for the CO, F/Sgt (Engineering) and such, was situated near the present Airport's entrance. The Orderly Room was at one time under the watchful eye of Sgt R. W. Knight with instrument and wireless shops nearby. Instrument repairs were one of the many tasks undertaken by WAAFs.

The TR9 radios were modified locally for better performance by Wireless Technician Cpl J. Harvey, who also fitted control column switches for easier operation.

Sleeping quarters for NCOs and airmen were Nissen huts on the airfield adjacent to Dispersal 1, along with 'O' Flight Commander's office. Officers used the Oatfield Wood Living Sites, but a number are known to have been billeted out in nearby Wrington and Churchill. Messes were initially shared with 3(P)AFU on the Communal Site.

S/L F. M. Beerling arrived from 20(P)AFU, Kidlington, on April 13th to take up duties as Senior Administration Officer.

6: *Further changes*

As a prelude to further residential changes, W/C R. J. Gosnell DFC, CO of 3 Flying Instructors School (FIS), Hullavington, attended a conference at Lulsgate on April 30th to discuss building progress and messing accommodation for the forthcoming arrival of his School, and further meetings were held during June and August.

3 (P)AFU Oxford I, ED287, was damaged beyond repair on May 17th while parked when hit by Oxford I, W6593, driven by Sgt C. T. C. Dibley at 0945, and the unit lost Oxford I, LX218, just after midnight on August 2nd, when it stalled and dived in at Quarry Farm, Wrington, killing the pilot and only occupant, Australian Sgt R. N. F. Brown; Oxford II AB771 was lost on August 23rd when the pilot failed to correct swing on take-off, the starboard wing dropped, and the aircraft crashed killing Sgt G. G. Barsky and Sgt N. E. M. Williams. Minor accidents during the year included Oxford I LB454, of 1540 BATF which taxied into 3(P)AFU's Oxford I, EB738, on August 28th, damaging only the aircraft.

On September 27th, 3(P)AFU ceased to use Lulsgate as a satellite, and from the 29th began using Southrop. Their place was taken by 3 FIS who moved in, along with a WAAF contingent, from Castle Combe and Babdown Farm, on October 1st. Although their HQ had been Hullavington, most of the flying had centered on the two satellites. Its task was the conversion of seasoned squadron pilots into Qualified Flying Instructors for OTUs.

The School was organised into Flights A to E with Oxford Is/IIs, Master IIs, and a few Master IIIs, (eg: W8456 to 16 FTS, 11/10/43, and W8692 to 15 MU at Wroughton, 14/10/43). No. 47 Course started the day they moved in, while 46 Course took their exams that afternoon. The CFI was S/L C. W. Thomas, and CO, W/C Gosnell, became Station Commander, taking up residence at Clappers.

Not all the amenities were complete when 3 FIS arrived, some sleeping units and other buildings did not come into use until the following March. Electricity and water had not been laid on to the WAAF site off Backwell Hill Road, and in the meantime hurricane lamps were used, water having to be fetched and heated on stoves which the girls took turns to light and keep stoked up.

There was a change of COs at the BATF on November 29th when

S/L B. E. Moody of 3(P)AFU swopped Units with S/L Gordon.

With the introduction of SBA, officials from British Overseas Airways Corporation (BOAC) paid a visit in December to discuss Lulsgate's possible use for training their Dakota and Liberator crews.

Since early May, BOAC's operations included a Dakota service (7M) to Lisbon and Gibraltar from their wartime base at Whitchurch, routing via Chivenor. Until then KLM had been operating one to Lisbon and Gibraltar on behalf of BOAC. The new service left Whitchurch at 16.15 GMT, arriving Chivenor 45 minutes later where it refuelled and waited until darkness before leaving at 22.00, arriving Lisbon at 05.00 GMT. The inaugural flight on May 11th in Dakota I, G-AGGI, had left Chivenor at 01.00, arriving at 08.00 in Lisbon. Departure for Gibraltar was made at 10.00 GMT, landing there at 12.00. The return flight initially routed via Chivenor, but was adjusted to a direct leg: Lisbon–Whitchurch, departing 23.00 GMT, arriving 06.00. During the summer a route was opened to Fez, this being replaced by Rabat by early September (Service 13M). On September 1st these services began operating from Lyneham direct to Lisbon, the return legs (8M and 14M) terminating at Whitchurch. Departures again began originating from Whitchurch on December 31st, but in certain adverse weather conditions arrangements were made to use Lulsgate by flying aircraft over light to top up with fuel and, exceptionally, embark passengers. By April 1944 the outbound routes were scheduled via St Mawgan.

The Lulsgate area saw a number of crashes during the War concerning allied aircraft not connected with the airfield. One such occurred on December 16th, 1943 when Photo Reconnaissance Spitfire PRIV, BS491, of 541 Squadron, crashed at Chelvey Farm, Backwell, in poor weather and burnt out. The aircraft was probably on a positioning flight from Gibraltar to Benson in Oxfordshire. The pilot, P/O R. Johnson, was killed.

One interesting visitor earlier in the year was Oxford I Ambulance, P8833, which arrived on January 20th before taking its patients on to Sussex the following day. This was the second of two Oxford Ambulances built by Airspeed, the other being P8832. Both served with 24 Squadron at Hendon.

On the last day of 1943 three Liberators returning from operations landed due to bad weather.

Despite the concentrated training programme, time was found for a variety of leisure activities. Passes allowed visits to Bristol, Weston, Clevedon and others, and mention has already been made of local public houses. Dances were organised, Barrow Gurney Hospital was one of the venues, as well as the Station itself which had its own band.

31

Sports were encouraged, and teams raised among students and staff to play local sides. The Weston Fire Service, for example, played a New Zealand cricket team during the summer of '43.

With 3 FIS and 1540 BATF firmly established at Lulsgate, 1944 was a typical year in the life of a wartime training airfield, with the usual spate of accidents, incidents, aircraft changes, and postings.

A new CFI, S/L R. E. Stevenson, took over from S/L Thomas on January 13th, to be replaced four days later by S/L M. M. Stephens DSO DFC.

Early in the year two of the BATF's Oxford Is were grounded for repair due to exposure: DF259 on January 28th, and V4223 on March 23rd. HM830/R arrived from Hullavington on February 16th as a replacement for the former.

On March 12th the under-carriage of V4224 collapsed while taxying, F/L Dodgson was the pilot but no one was hurt.

After only a month back in service the unfortunate DF259 was again being repaired after carburettor icing caused a loss of power to both engines during take-off on April 1st; again the accident was without casualties. This aircraft eventually went to 3 FIS who also had their share of accidents during the year.

On February 15th, F/O L. W. R. Rogers became the first 3 FIS instructor to be killed, along with his student, F/O F. Garvey, when their Oxford I, LW776, crashed at 10.30 shortly after take-off from Whitchurch. Weak mixture was selected, and both engines cut out at very low altitude.

March 5th saw Master II, DM295, force land at Weston Zoyland, and four days later another Master II, DM241, was damaged by a contractor's lorry on the ground at Lulsgate.

Oxford I, HN203, was damaged at Whitchurch at 09.40 on March 23rd when the starboard engine failed on overshoot. During the subsequent precautionary landing, the aircraft trundled off the end of the runway into a hidden ditch. The instructor, F/O H. H. V. Roots, and his Canadian pupil, P/O R. E. Erickson, were unhurt.

At 16.00 on March 26th, Oxford I, ED271, tipped on its nose after landing too far into the small airfield at Yate, finishing up on rough ground. The pilot was F/O C. Phillipson-Stow.

At Lulsgate the undercarriage of 'E' Flight Oxford II, V3511, was inadvertently raised in dispersal on April 14th at 12.30. The pilot, F/L A. H. Pye, meant to select 'flaps up'. This was a common error with Oxfords as the two controls were situated close together low down on the central console between the pilots.

Master II, EM355, force landed after engine failure just west of Bleadon and Uphill railway station at 11.00 on May 8th. Canadian,

3 Sec. 2 Plt. 6 Comp. 7th Som. Batt. H.G. 1944 (photograph: Mrs L. Pearce).

F/O T. J. Decourcy acting as 1st pilot, and F/O R. A. Miller, were injured.

On May 12th at 12.30, Oxford I, V3953, overshot on landing and struck the boundary fence as a result of excessive speed on touchdown. The pilot was Sgt C. J. Norgrove.

While landing in bad visibility during a thunderstorm and a crosswind on the wrong runway, Oxford II, V3862, crashed through a hedge at 16.45 on May 30th. New Zealander F/O A. G. Mayfield was acting as 1st pilot, accompanied by Canadian P/O D. T. Cook.

On D-Day, June 6th, at 09.40, 'A' Flight's Oxford I, L4616, crashed near the Waggon and Horses killing F/O Roots and his student, F/L P. M. Cadman, after the port engine and wing caught fire during circuit training. Jim Vowles of nearby Freemans Farm, Barrow Gurney, was first on the scene having witnessed the accident. Due to the intense fire there was no hope for those on board, but he did salvage one of the main wheels which spun clear. He had to make out a report on what he saw, and whilst at the airfield was invited to fly in an Oxford. He recalls the flight well, seeing his farm from the air for the first time, and even remembers the aircraft's number, 67. He managed to keep the wheel which, with its tyre, has miraculously survived the last 45 years, despite being put to use on the farm. Mr Vowles remembers Canadians coming to the farm and asking for milk and *onions!* The airfield also provided willing helpers at harvest time.

At 15.30 on June 20th the tail unit of Master II, DM295, broke

33

completely away from the fuselage due to a tail-wheel failure after a heavy landing. This was partially caused by a poor aerodrome surface. F/Sgt King and Sgt J. Filliol were on board.

Whilst on finals at Whitchurch on July 10th at 15.30, Master II, W9067, hit a USAAC Stinson Sentinel. The Master caught fire on crashing and both the instructor, F/O E. H. Marsh, and his pupil, F/O E. A. H. Lawrence, were injured.

On July 24th Oxford I, V3243, struck EB905 while taxying, causing slight damage.

Oxford I, BG245, hit a Drem lighting post while making an approach during night circuits in poor visibility at 01.50 on July 31st. Neither the instructor, P/O E. W. Smith, and the Canadian pupil, P/O M. H. Sims, were hurt in the subsequent forced landing ¼ mile east of the field.

On August 11th at 14.45, Master II, EM297, belly-landed damaging the propellor, flaps, and engine, after the pilot failed to lower the under-carriage W/O W. A. Savage was the Canadian pupil, and his instructor, F/O E. H. Marsh.

Master II, AZ605, crashed into the sea west of Clevedon on August 21st, killing the two student pilots, Lt A. J. Hunt RNVR and Sub/Lt D. L. Olds, a New Zealander of the RNZNVR, while on a daylight exercise.

The port engine of Oxford I, P8899, cut due to fuel starvation on the downwind leg of the circuit on November 14th. The under-carriage was lowered but not locked down in time, and a belly-landing parallel to the runway was executed at 12.15. 1st pilot, F/O J. A. Newberry, and F/O J. L. Kennedy, were uninjured.

There were many other minor incidents of one sort or another during the year, some involving the following aircraft: May: Oxford Is, LW744 (9th) and HN521 (12th). June: Oxford I, LW868 (30th). August: Oxford I, AT793 (14th).

As an indication of the number of aircraft based at Lulsgate in 1944, during April, 3 FIS alone had 50 Oxfords and 10 Masters.

One of the minor incidents referred to involved Oxford I, ED257, on August 26th at the North Stoke RLG. Situated on Lansdown above Bath, this Relief Landing Ground had been assessed as suitable for operations by 3 FIS's CFI on May 7th the previous year, although it was traversed by a public right-of-way which could prove rather hair-raising, especially at weekends when it appeared half Bath used to come up and watch the flying! On one Saturday in 1945, A. H. Thomsett, F/O with 3 FIS, recalls someone opening the door of his Oxford and climbing in for a joy-ride just as he was about to take-off!

Lulsgate's hard runways were unusual for a training airfield,

34

although its all-the-year-round operating capability was hampered by the high elevation exposing it to any bad weather moving up the Bristol Channel, especially low cloud. During the autumn of 1944, strong winds were a problem, causing damage to aircraft parked in the open.

In contrast to 1540 BATF's letters, eg Oxford I, NM243/O, 3 FIS had large individual aircraft numbers painted in a similar position on the fuselage adjacent to the roundel, both numbers and letters being White or Sky, eg Master IIs: EM297/4, AZ605/7, and DM115/11; Oxford Is: EB865/25, EB905/27, LW868/29, HN203/30, V3953/33, HN521/41, ED271/43, ED257/48, BG245/54, V3243/76, and HM644/78; and Oxford II, V3511/52. These numbers were not confined to the one aircraft, as planes went out of service, changed units, and so on, they were frequently re-allocated, eg 27 was carried by both EB905 and another 3 FIS Oxford I, V3981.

In February 1944, BATFs introduced a further yellow triangle on top of the fuselage behind the cockpit, followed in June by black triangles outboard of the underwing roundels.

From May 1944, Oxfords began appearing with side panels of engine cowlings in yellow, as well as the outer four feet of the wingtip upper surfaces, plus a yellow fuselage band with a centreline passing through the roundel's centre, and its width being that of the blue ring's outer diameter. For BATF Oxfords these were proposed as an alternative to their triangles, but many carried them in addition.

Visitors during 1944 included a USAAF C-47, 224134, which landed with engine trouble on February 20th.

Another American incident in the Lulsgate area occurred on March 14th when a Liberator in a grey scheme with US markings en route from North Africa is believed to have run out of fuel trying to land at Lulsgate in foggy conditions and scythed into a wood on the hill overlooking Compton Martin, breaking off its tail before hitting a large oak tree on Hazel Manor Farm. A number of the crew were killed.

A Liberator, callsign 'Hostess Able', diverted in after a 'Darky' call on May 30th. There was thunderstorm activity in the area at the time.

A Fortress made a refuelling stop on June 20th at 14.00 after operations in which it sustained slight battle damage resulting in a small flak hole below the 2nd pilot's window on the starboard side, fortunately no one was injured.

As a result of another Darky call, this time on August 2nd, two Dakotas, callsigns '777' and '301', arrived in formation at 02.24 out of a 4-500 feet cloudbase. 301's radio was very poor.

Eight Darky calls were received during the month of August, and assistance offered to four.

On Sunday, September 17th, Horsa glider, RJ113, crashed near Paulton killing the 23 soldiers on board including two glider pilots. It broke away from Stirling IV, LK148/R, (Australian pilot, F/L G. Liggins), from 299 Squadron at Keevil, while en route to Arnhem.

A Westland Welkin, DX308, force landed with engine trouble on September 18th while en route from the manufacturers at Yeovil to 22 MU (Maintenance Unit), Silloth, for storage.

Halifax V, LL126, from 1662 Heavy Conversion Unit (HCU), Blyton, crashed on night exercise at Long Ashton on October 21st. The Polish crew of seven were killed.

During the latter part of the year three Wellingtons were among the diversions, all with engine trouble. One landed with its port engine u/s on September 10th, followed ten days later by a Mk.III, DF594, of 22 OTU, Wellesbourne Mountford. Finally, a 27 OTU Wellington, 'UJ-I', from Lichfield, flown by F/Sgt Mcleod, arrived on the night of November 25th with a starboard engine failure. All visitors were assured of a very hospitable welcome from the Station.

Darky was the code-word for a method of HF communication with aircraft lost or in distress. From 1941 onwards the RAF installed short range TR9D HF radios at airfields for this purpose. A simple transmitter/receiver on 6440Hz with a range of around 10 miles was used, being operated in the air by the pilot, and on the ground by WAAFs with associated loudspeakers. For a known aircraft callsign the ground station would use the word 'Koska', and for an unknown, 'Neemo'. Where coverage by the RAF was poor, the Royal Observer Corps joined the scheme during the autumn of 1942.

Although none were Darky sites, the nearest ROC posts to Lulsgate were Long Ashton and Winscombe, with others at Avonmouth, Portishead, Clevedon, Weston-super-Mare, Chilton, and West Harptree.

The airfield came within 23 Group, Bristol ROC, with Group HQ originally in Little King Street until 1943, then Worcester Terrace. Group Commandant 1943-45 was Observer Commander F. C. Lockyer. The Group in turn came within Western Area Command whose HQ moved from Gloucester to 10 Group Fighter Command's HQ at Rudloe Manor near Bath during 1942. Commandants were Air Commodore E. A. D. Masterman CB CMG AFC to 1943, then Observer Captain J. W. Saunders until 1945. The distinction 'Royal' was bestowed in 1941, and blue battledress was issued during 1942/43, superseding the original boiler-suits. Another ROC code-name probably familiar to aircrews was 'Granite'. This referred to sites equipped with red flares for warning aircraft of high ground. The majority of such sites in Somerset were situated in the Blackdown, Brendon, Polden, and Quantock Hills areas.

Many instructors continued at Lulsgate under 3 FIS after 3(P)AFU had moved out. Flight Commanders during 1943/44 included F/L S. B. Wills (of the tobacco family): one-time OC 'A' Flight; F/L J. F. Hatton: OC 'B' Flight; F/L Trinder: OC 'Singles' Flight; plus F/L's K. Howlett and R. M. Pugh. Other known instructors at the time, including other possible Flight Commanders, were F/Ls Culverwell and Sellers, F/Os Hancock, Jones, Lynskey, Marsh, Roberts, and Stevens. 25 year old S/L G. F. Morley-Mower DFC AFC also served with 3 FIS from April 30th, 1944 until June 11th, 1945 becoming Assistant CFI. He stayed in Wrington and drove to Lulsgate every day on his Norton motor-cycle. On Mess dance nights his young wife used to tuck up her long evening dress and ride pillion! S/L W. D. K. Franklin joined 3 FIS on January 20th, 1944 instructing in various capacities including OC '1 Squ' and Deputy CFI.

Favourite mount of F/O A. J. Angus, a member of 'A' Flight both with 3 FIS and later 7 FIS, was Oxford I, LW775/71.

F/L 'Lofty' Wills was so tall that he presented an odd sight when flying the Station Magister with his head and shoulders way above the open cockpit!

F/L R. Bouts was a 3 FIS instructor on the Link Trainer. The instrument section during the year ending January 1945 came under F/Sgt V. F. Griffith. One of the Accounts Officers 1943–45 was T. H. Williams, another being F/L S. 'Sammy' Hughes.

W/C Gosnell was posted to 19 OTU on July 11th 1944, and W/C T. B. de la Beresford DSO DFC became the new CO of 3 FIS. Known as 'Barny', he had a dog called 'Rusty', and was a keen huntin', shootin', and fishin' man. His father was a well known King's Councillor. R. A. E. Allen remembers as a young F/O being met and welcomed to Lulsgate in November 1944 by W/C Beresford mounted on his horse.

Harvard IIbs began replacing Masters during the summer of 1944. In January 1945 the 'Singles' Flight was housed in a blister hanger adjacent to the control tower, along with the Station Maggie. Harvard examples: FX199/1, FX416/5.

A 'Sandra' cone was made available in August 1944 with the co-operation of local searchlight units to assist pilots in finding the airfield.

In 1941 the standard procedure to obtain searchlight homing when in distress or in need of assistance was to circle for at least two minutes, fire the colours of the day, and flash a series of dots on the navigation lights. The searchlight unit for its part would depress their beam horizontally in the direction of the airfield for 30 seconds, then elevate it to 45°, then lower it again, three times in succession, finally leaving the beam in the horizontal position for a further 30 seconds. This exercise was repeated until the aircraft was safely on course, when the beam was left horizontal for two minutes until the engine(s) had died away. Canopies of searchlights were introduced and put up over certain airfields, accompanied by signal rockets. S/L F. T. K. Bullmore, Senior Flying Control officer at Boscombe Down, was responsible for organising co-ordination between Royal Observer Corps posts and the various Commands and searchlight batteries. He also acquired a large number of searchlights from Anti-Aircraft Command, and distributed them to various airfields to improve canopy patterns, as well as to other RAF and RoC sites for homing and gap-filling. These canopy lights were originally known as RoC Lights, but this was changed to the more familiar code-name, Sandra.

As previously mentioned, BOAC used the facilities at Lulsgate on a number of occasions during the latter part of the War for training.

An incident of some interest that happened shortly before D-Day is related by F/O Hardman. A flight of USAAF C-47s, each towing a glider, passed overhead in a southerly direction. Later it was reported that a glider had broken its tow and landed on the moors a few miles away. Soon afterwards a C-47 landed at Lulsgate. After stopping near the tower, a ramp was lowered and a jeep, complete with ground crew, poles, and a large coil of rope, drove out leaving the Station in the direction of the stranded glider. About 45 minutes later the C-47 took off, and pilots airborne in their Oxfords reported that the ground crew had looped the two ends of the rope around the hook of the glider and elevated the middle of it over the two poles well above ground level. When the C-47 arrived on the scene it was trailing a cable with a hook on the end which engaged the loop of rope, accelerating the glider into the air. The combination then continued their delayed flight. Back at Lulsgate a C-47 touched down just as the jeep and crew returned, the ramp was lowered, jeep loaded, and the aircraft departed to complete a very slick operation.

On December 1st, 1944 personnel at Lulsgate totalled 1,043:

RAF:	128 Officers	125 Senior NCOs	572 Other Ranks
WAAF:	4 "	10 " "	204 " "

7: *Running down*

One of the last 'incidents' of the war occurred at 10.30 on January 21st 1945 while F/Sgt K. G. Richards was taxi-ing Oxford I, DF259, when he failed to see a tractor crossing his path. He and his passenger were not hurt, but the aircraft was slightly damaged.

Another on February 2nd saw Oxford I, EB905, piloted by F/O W. D. J. Sedgewick and F/O W. F. McElwain, a New Zealander, experienced excessive vibration immediately after take-off, power was reduced and the aircraft belly-landed at 16.10. On the same day S/L W. A. Howell became CFI of 3 FIS, replacing S/L M. M. Stephens.

1540 BATF moved to Weston Zoyland on February 6th with eight aircraft. The move had commenced the previous day but was delayed due to bad weather, and on arrival they even found the Link Trainer room waterlogged!

The OTU Flight (including 26 OTU Course) from 7 FIS, Upavon, was transferred to 3 FIS on February 23rd, becoming 'F' Flight. The Road Party for Lulsgate, with 58 airmen and women, was under the command of F/L R. M. Pugh, and a second, consisting of 18 airmen and women, with F/O A. S. H. Chalmers in charge, moved to Hullavington. F/O Chalmers lost his way and stopped a chauffeur-driven Daimler to ask directions. He found it contained Her Majesty Queen Mary, who was most amused! The Air Party for Lulsgate, under F/L W. A. Wilkinson, consisted of the following 13 Oxfords:

Serial	Captain	Passengers
BG149	F/L W. A. Wilkinson	F/O C. W. Barnett
HN211	F/O D. J. Carmichael	F/O C. E. Thompson
DF254	F/O A. J. Angus	F/O S. Garside/
		F/O D. R. McKenzie
HM696	F/O F. J. Ballam	F/O M. J. O'Loughlin
BM832	Lt G. Meyer	F/O E. Barton
HN121	F/O M. G. Johnson	F/O O.G. Thomas
HM851	F/L R. C. Davie	F/O J. Clark
HM731	F/O J. S. Hiddleston	F/O G. R. Hildane

MP409	F/O F. E. H. Millar	F/O W. H. Novick
HM614	F/O R. H. Taylor	F/O J. H. F. White
V3981	F/O R. B. King	F/O T. C. Waugh
HN667	F/O J. D. Movat	F/O G. E. Colley
BG167	F/O A. M. Bourne	F/O R. D. Jennings

All the Oxfords were Mk.I's except Mk.II, BM832. At Lulsgate, BG149 to HM614 inclusive are known to have been numbered '10' to '20', omitting '13'. V3981 at one time carried number '27', HN667 numbers '33' and '67', and BG167 number '68'.

OTU Instructors

F/L R. O. Whitehead	On leave to February 25th
F/L W. A. Wilkinson	By air
F/L H. F. C. Joy	Sick
F/L R. M. Pugh	By road — Service transport
F/O A. S. H. Chalmers	By road to Hullavington, then to Lulsgate
F/O D. J. Carmichael	By air (Canadian)
F/O A. J. Angus	By air
F/O F. J. Ballam	By air

Course Pilots (all by air)

Lt G. Meyer	F/O M. J. O'Loughlin
F/O M. G. Johnson	F/O E. Barton
F/L R. C. Davie	F/O O. G. Thomas
F/O J. S. Hiddleston	F/O J. Clark
F/O F. E. H. Millar	F/O G. R. Hildane
F/O R. H. Taylor	F/O W. H. Novick
F/O R. B. King	F/O J. H. F. White
F/O C. W. Barnett	F/O T. C. Waugh
F/O J. D. Movat	F/O R. D. Jenning
F/O C. E. Thompson	F/O A. M. Bourne
F/O S. Garside	F/O D. R. McKenzie
	F/O G. E. Colley

F/O F. H. Dongate and F/O D. A. Richards by F/O Dongate's car.

'F' Flight was commanded by F/L R. M. Pugh who was awarded an AFC while at Lulsgate.

W/C Beresford was posted to 3 PDC on March 5th, his place being taken by W/C E. K. 'Pluto' Piercy DFC, who was to marry the Met Officer, the most attractive girl on the Station!

Numbered among other 3 FIS instructors around this time were F/L D. A. C. Hunt who commanded 'A' Flight; F/L's J. F. Hatton and J. Barrien both of whom at one time commanded 'B' Flight; F/L Overton; F/L T. Hodgson ('A' Flight); and on the Link Trainer, F/Sgt Bryant.

F/O 'Johnny' Chalmers and F/O 'Tony' Angus (both of whom were eventually promoted to F/L) owned a 1932 Austin 7 which they

Front Row. Left to Right: F/L Nyles. F/O Davies. F/L Henry. S/O Dickman. S/O Simpson. F/L Beighton. S/L Lamb. S/L Beorling. S/L Bagall. I/O Chater. F/O Rankin. S/L Franklin. F/L Short. F/L Pearson. S/L Dinsdale. S/O Butt. S/O Oitsdold. S/O Haye. F/O Pritchard. F/L Harland. F/L Stephenson.

Second Row. Left to Right: F/O Palmer. F/L Roome. F/L Russell. F/L Lodge. F/L Pinney. F/L Faulkner. F/L Brinkley. F/L Spain. F/L Tester. F/L Pugh. F/L Hunt. F/L King. F/L Stacre. F/L Litchfield. F/L Tattersall. F/L Chalmers. F/L Whitehead. F/L Angus. F/L Stoop. F/O Allen. W/O Wall. F/O Pecklatch.

Back Row. Left to Right: F/O Lockie. F/L Widger. F/L Miller. F/O Stacey. F/L Gillies. F/L Yellowlees. F/L Phillips. F/L Medimos. F/O Hawes. F/O Jewitt. F/L Hall. F/L Webb. F/L O'Brien. F/L Butt. F/O Overton. F/O Mort. F/O Miller. F/O Roberts. F/O Waldron.

Staff, Lulsgate 1945 (photograph: A.E. Tattersall).

successfully 'rolled' near Churchill returning from a local pub, luckily with little damage either to car or occupants which included a couple of WAAFs! Chalmers became Mess Secretary at Lulsgate, a post he held until its closure.

May 8th ended Europe's War.

W/C Piercy was posted to 23 Group HQ on June 23rd, and W/C H.A. Chater from 20(P)AFU at Kidlington, Oxford, where he was OC Flying Wing became the new CO. W/C Hugh Chater resided in the CO's single quarters hut behind the Officer's Mess on the Communal Site, which he eventually had extended to accommodate his wife towards the end of his stay at Lulsgate. S/L 'Bill' Howell continued as CFI with S/L W.D.K. Franklin as his Deputy (Derek Franklin was another who kept a dog, his was 'Persil' white).

July 18th saw the closure of 3 FIS, and from that day the airfield became a satellite for 7 FIS's Oxfords and Harvards organised into Flights 'A' to 'D', and utilising ex-3 FIS aircraft and personnel. W/C Chater became Detachment Commander, while S/L Howell and S/L Franklin stayed on in their original 3 FIS roles.

Aircraft examples: Oxford Is: HM696/14 and PH512/37; Harvard IIbs: FX199/1 and FT361/4.

Officers at Lulsgate, July 1945

W/C H. A. Chater	Commanding Officer
Flt/O Heather Rankin	I/C WAAF's
S/L F. M. Beerling	Senior Admin. Officer
S/L R. A. Dimsdale	Col. Turner's Dept. AM, C&D Area 10
S/L W. A. Howell	CFI
S/L W. D. K. Franklin	Dep./CFI
S/L Lane	OC, Engineering

F/Ls:

A. J. Angus
L. G. Batt
A. S. H. Chalmers
Faulkner
Gillies
Hall
L. L. Harland ——— Principles of Flight, Ground School
Hawes
Henry
D. A. C. Hunt ——— OC 'A' Flight
R. King
Leigh
O. Leighton
Litchfield
MacInnes
J. Miller

Q. St Leger Myles —————— MO, arrived April 15th 1945 from India
    O'Brien
    Overton
J. C. Pearson
    Phillips
A. Pinney
R. M. Pugh —————— OC 'B' Flight
    Roome
    Russell
    Short
    Spain
J. H. Steere —————— OC 'C' Flight
    Stephenson
R. C. Stoop
A. E. Tattersall —————— Senior Flying Control Officer
    Tester
'Tommy' Trinder
    J. Webb —————— OC 'D' Flight
R. O. Whitehead
    Widger
    Yellowlees

F/Os:

R. A. E. Allen	Palmer
Davies	Pendleton
Jewitt	Pritchard
Leckie	Roberts
Miller	Stacey
Mort	Waldron

W/Os:

P. Wall

Sec/O's:
(WAAF)

Clissold	Hutt
Ditcham	Mayo
P. Simpson ————	Senior Met Officer

During July a Spitfire landed at Lulsgate with engine trouble. It was test flown by W/C Chater on July 24th before returning to its base at Chivenor. Serial unknown, but it carried the letter B.

Other visitors during the year included a USAAF Mustang, callsign 'WW12', on July 15th, en route Northern Ireland to Cambridge which diverted in after being blown off course and short of fuel.

The first jets to land at Lulsgate were three Meteors on September 6th which were short of fuel and unable to make Colerne.

BOAC continued to use the airfield at odd times for training, including night landings. On August 8th one of their Yorks arrived from Hurn returning the same day.

A Battle of Britain Display was held on September 15th when the Station was thrown open to the public. The weather, unfortunately, was not good with Lulsgate's famous low cloud restricting flying. Even so a Lancaster appeared, managing to land on one of the shorter runways, and F/L Whitehead, with F/L Chalmers as pupil, carried out a circuits and landings demonstration in an Oxford, while Whitehead's instructional patter was transmitted over the public address system.

The PTI Sgt in the Sports Section from June 1945 until closure was H. Baldock, who also doubled as a drummer in the Station band. The officer i/c at one time was F/O Balderstone. During the same period J. Collins was in the Post Office, and R. Deverson the Orderly Room.

At any RAF station there were the inevitable Mess parties, and as has been briefly shown Lulsgate was no exception. At such entertainments in the Officer's Mess, F/L Widger, who was blessed with a completely bald head and rather thin legs, used to don ballet skirt and practise his entrechats on the table! He was also a brilliant conjurer, and a member of the Magic Circle.

S/L Franklin left on January 2nd 1946, his place being taken by S/L H. Gandy DFC AFC who had joined 7 FIS on December 28th 1945. He had served with 3 FIS as an instructor back in 1942.

W/C Chater became CFI with 7 FIS at Upavon on February 18th 1946, replacing W/C J. L. Walters AFC, and S/L Gandy became Detachment CFI.

On January 22nd, Ramsbury became a satellite of Upavon, and plans were made to move the 7 FIS Detachment there. Arrangements to disperse the WAAFs were finalised on February 27th, and the last left on March 30th. During that month BOAC and Ministry of Civil Aviation officials inspected certain facilities and equipment for possible purchase.

Flying training ceased on April 15th, and two days later packing started for Little Rissington, the Ramsbury plans having been dropped.

While preparations continued it was decided on the 22nd to split the move and involve South Cerney. The Advance Party left for Little Rissington on April 24th, the Main Party leaving on May 2nd when all flying ceased. The last aircraft to go were half-a-dozen Oxfords. Colour schemes changed to overall yellow then silver with yellow bands, and new black code letters began to appear, eg Oxford I, HM696 FDL-F, and Harvard IIb, FX199 FDM-P.

Harvard IIb, FT281 (photograph: IWM ATP 13216E).

Junkers Ju. 88A-6, 4D + DL, at Lulsgate (photograph: Kenneth S. West).

During May, 7 FIS were to become the nucleus of a reformed Central Flying School.

The Rear Party left for Little Rissington and South Cerney on May 7th, and the following day the airfield was reduced to Care and Maintenance. All equipment worth salvaging was removed, and on October 25th, 1946 the airfield was officially abandoned.

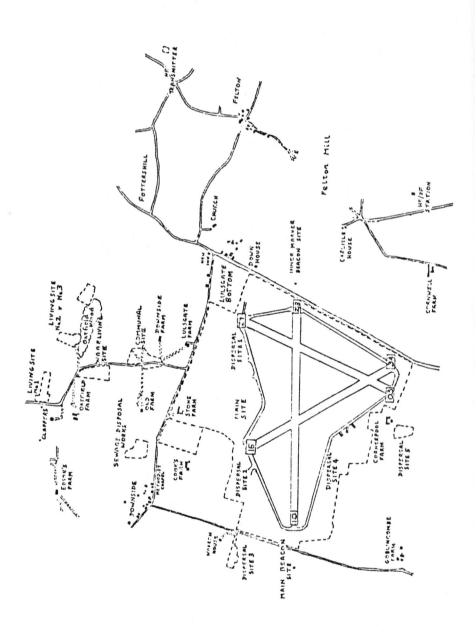

R.A.F LULSGATE BOTTOM

Site Plans

Key

TEMPORARY BRICK BUILDINGS INDICATED THUS		T.B.
CONCRETE BUILDINGS " "		C.
STEEL " " "		ST.
NISSEN HUTTING " "		N.
SECO " " "		S.
LAING " " "		L.
ROMNEY " " "		R.
HANDCRAFT (ASBESTOS) HUTTING " "		A.
CORRUGATED IRON " " "		C.I.

MAIN SITE

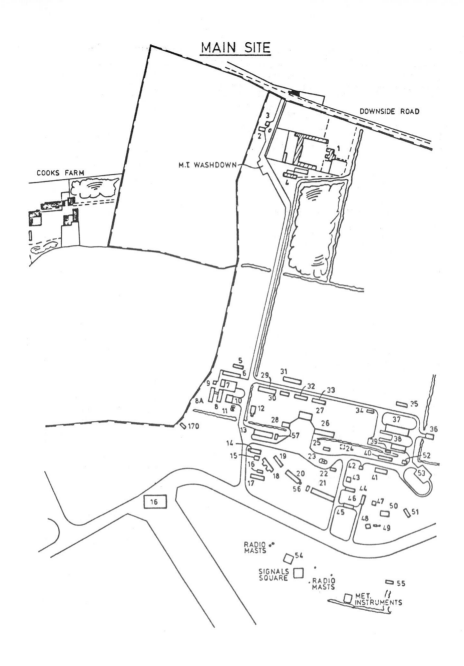

DOWNSIDE ROAD

COOKS FARM

M.T. WASHDOWN

RADIO MASTS

SIGNALS SQUARE

RADIO MASTS

MET. INSTRUMENTS

MAIN SITE

Bldg.No.	Building	Constn.	Dwg. No.
1	STATION OFFICES (OLD BLDGS "STONE FARM" ADAPTED	BK & STONE	12 WA/LG570
2	POST OFFICE (30'x18')	MAGNET HUT	734/44
3	GUARD HUT (12'x12')	T.B.	NIL
4	BOWSER MAINTENANCE DEPOT	T.B.	202/42
5	GUARD HOUSE	T.B.	4833/41
6	A.M.W.D. PAINT STORE (16'-0'-NISSEN) 76'x16'	N.	
7	" WORKS SERVICE BUILDING 36'x16'	N.	7393/41
8	" CLERK OF WORKS OFFICE 50'x16'	T.	NIL
9A	" STORES 60'x19'7"	S.	12WA/TDS951
9	" LATRINE 15'x10'	T.B.	NIL
10	AGRICULTURAL IMPLEMENT SHED	-	12 WA/TDS 563
11	SUB-STATION KIOSK	BRICK	12648/40
12	LINK TRAINER (1-COMPT)	A.	12 WA/LG 616
13	ARMOURY	T.B.	4832/41
14	LINK TRAINER AND OFFICES (1-COMPT) 40'x15'	T.	12WA/LG571
15	STATIC WATER TANK 7000 GAL.	C.	12 WA/TDS155
16	CYCLE SHELTER	LOCAL	NIL
17	OFFICES AND LECTURE ROOM 60'x18'	L.	12WA/LG571
18	LINK TRAINER OFFICE AND WORKSHOP (2-COMPT)	L.	12WA/LG484
19	GAS DEFENCE CENTRE	T.B.	48/40
20	LECTURE ROOMS 60'x18'	L	12 WA/LG571
21	SQUADRON OFFICE (AS FLYING WING OFFICE)	T.B.	4831/41
22	TECHNICAL LATRINE (W.A.A.F.)	"	4026/41
23	M.T. PETROL INSTALLATION 1000 GAL.	"	489/41
24	BULK OIL COMPOUND 20'x20'	WIRE ENC.	15932/40
25	TECHNICAL LATRINE (R.A.F.)	T.B.	4830/41
26	MAINTENANCE AND SQUADRON OFFICE	L & S	9106/43
27	M.T. GARAGE (4 BAY)	T.B.	12775/41
28	M.T. OFFICE		
29	NAVIGATION LECTURE ROOM BLOCK (72'x24')	S.	7974 "
30	NAVIGATION AND SIGNALS INSTRUCTORS COMMON ROOM	S.	" "
31	NAVIGATION LECTURE ROOM BLOCK (72'x24')	S.	" "
32	AIRCRAFT & SHIP RECOGNITION & CINE GUN ASSESSING RM'	S.	9975/42
33	INTELLIGENCE LIBRARY AND QUIET ROOM (60x19'7")	S.	" "
34	TECHNICAL LATRINE (R.A.F.)	T.B.	9026/41
35	GAS CLOTHING AND RESPIRATOR STORE 1120	"	12409/41
36	BATTERY CHARGING ROOM	"	15086/41
37	MAIN STORE (96'x35')	R.	5539/42
38	" " (60'x28')	T.B.	12WA/LG631
39	CYCLE SHELTER	LOCAL	NIL
40	LUBRICANT AND INFLAMMABLES STORE	T.B.	4833/41
41	PARACHUTE STORE	"	10825/42
42	SALT STORE 10'x10'	"	NIL
43	STATIC WATER TANK 7000 GAL.	C.	12WA/TDS155
44	FIRE PARTY AND WORKSHOP	A.	12 WA/LGS 87
45	FLOODLIGHT TRAILER AND TRACTOR SHED	T.B.	12411/41
46	FIRE TENDER SHELTER	"	5352/42
47	SPEECH BROADCASTING BUILDING	BRICK	5648/41
48	FIRE SECTION (ORIG'Y WATCH OFFICE, DWG 3156/41)	"	
49	SLEEVE STREAMER MAST.	S.T.	5749/36
50	INSTRUCTIONAL OPERATIONS ROOM (24'x36')	S.	2078/43
51	PYROTECHNIC STORE (30'x18')	T.B.	NIL
52	TRANSFORMER PLINTH	BLAST WALLS	"
53	FUEL COMPOUND (54'x54')	WIRE ENCL	178/41
54	CONTROL TOWER (WATCH OFFICE)	BRICK	12779/41
55	BATTLE HEADQUARTERS	"	3329/41
56-57	CYCLE SHELTER	LOCAL	NIL
170	TRANSFORMER PLINTH (BLAST WALL)		NIL

49

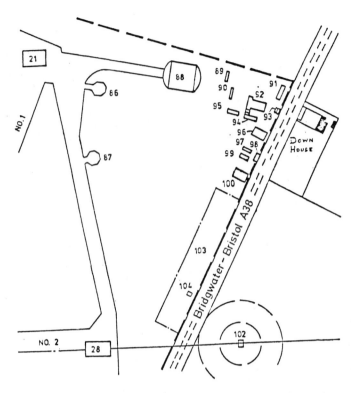

Bldg.No.	Building		Constn.	Dwg. No.
85-87	HARDSTANDING			12 WA/TDS358
88	HANGAR - BLISTER DOUBLE E-O		S.T.	12532/41
89	LATRINE	(36'x 6')		NIL
90	FLIGHT STORE HUT AND W.A.A.F. LATRINE	(40'x 9')	T. & T.B.	"
91	STORE	(50'x 18')	T.	"
92	" AND AIRMEN'S LATRINE		T.	"
93	TRANSFORMER PLINTH			"
94	ELECTRICAL INSTRUMENT AND WIRELESS ROOM	(50'x 18')	T.	12 WA/LG560
95	FLIGHT OFFICE AND ORDERLY ROOM	(50'x 18')	T.	" "
96	HANGAR - BLISTER (STANDARD)		T. & C.I.	12494/41
97	LINK TRAINER 1- COMPT.	(36'x16')	N.	12 WA/LG681
98	DEFENCE UNIT. KITCHEN ETC.		T. & COR: 1	NIL
99	STORE HUT	(36'x 16')	N	10024/41
100	HANGAR - BLISTER (STANDARD)		T. & C.I.	12494/41
102	INNER MARKER (B.A. SYSTEM)			M & E 11503/41
103	FUEL COMPOUND		WIRE ENCL	NIL
104	TOOL HOUSE TYPE 'B' (8'x 8')		T. B.	"

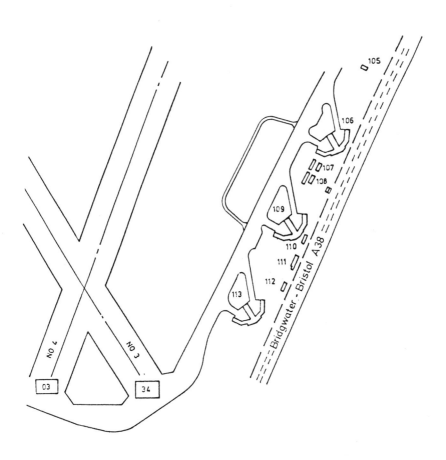

Bldg.No	Building		Constn.	Dwg. No.
105	S.A.A. STORE	(24'x16')		12725/41
106	AIRCRAFT PEN			7151/41
107	FLIGHT OFFICES	(16'N)	N	13214/41
108	TRANSFORMER PLINTH			NIL
109	AIRCRAFT PEN			7151/41
110	DISPERSAL LATRINE		T.B.	9026/41
111	SLEEPING SHELTER	(FOR 33)	BRICK	11049/41
112	DRYING ROOMS	(16'N)	N	13214/41
113	AIRCRAFT PEN			7151/41

Communal Site

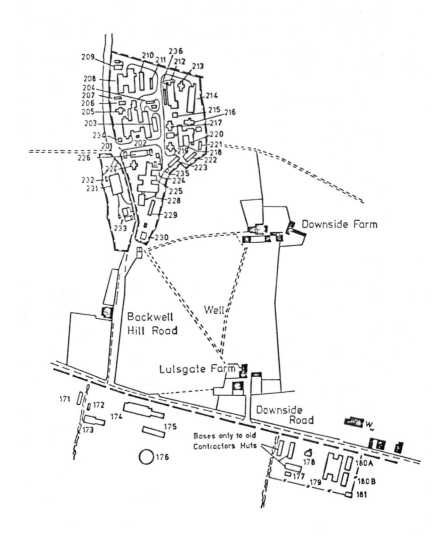

Bldg.No	Building	Constn.	Dwg. No.
201	PICKET POST (WITH PROPHYLACTIC ROOM)	T.B.	4830/41
202	DINING ROOM - FOR 709 (469 AIRMEN, 240 AIRWOMEN)	"	4837/41
203	STATIC WATER TANK 20,000 GALS.	C	12 WA/TDS 155
204	RATION STORE (FOR 709) WITH BUTCHERS PREP. ROOM	T.B. & S	4837/41
205	AIR RAID SHELTER - BLAST (FOR 50)		2360/41
206	FAT RENDERING PLANT HOUSE (18'-6" x 12'6")	'POLE	NIL
207	AIR RAID SHELTER - STANTON (FOR 50)		A.M. SUPPLY
208	INSTITUTE - FOR 709 (469 AIRMEN, 240 AIRWOMEN)	T.B.	4838/41
209	N.A.A.F.I. STAFF QUARTERS	T.B. & S	" - "
210	GAMES, READING & WRITING ROOM (FOR INSTITUTE) (72'x24')	S	9101/43
211	LATRINE BLOCK. R.A.F.	T.B.	4835/41
212	DECONTAM: CENTRE & OFFICERS SHOWERS. K.M. (FOR 700)	BRICK	13843/40
213	AIRRAID SHELTER - BLAST (FOR 50)		2360/41
214	AIRMEN'S SHOWERS & ABLUTIONS, W.A.A.F. LATS & ABLUTIONS	T.B.	4835/41
215	WATER TANK - HIGH LEVEL 30,000 GALS.	ST.	20/41
216-217	AIR RAID SHELTER - BLAST (FOR 50)		2360/41
218	SERGEANTS MESS FOR 123 (116 R.A.F. 7 W.A.A.F. SERGTS)	T.B. & S	4836/41
219	AIR RAID SHELTER - BLAST (FOR 50)		2360/41
220	BOILER HOUSE TO SERGEANTS MESS	T.B.	9100/43
221	SERGEANTS SHOWERS & LATRINES	" .	4835/41
222	BARBERS, TAILORS & SHOEMAKERS SHOP (48'x19'-7")	S	6558/43
223	M.I. HUT & DENTAL SURGERY	T.B.	3627/41
224	OFFICERS BATH HOUSE	"	4835/41
225	OFFICERS MESS FOR 143 (138 R.A.F. 5 W.A.A.F. OFFICERS)	T.B. & S	4834/41
226	GROCERY & LOCAL PRODUCE STORE	T.B.	4838/41
227	AIR RAID SHELTER - BLAST (FOR 50)		2360/41
228	COMMANDING OFFICERS QUARTERS (46'x 19'-7")	S	4287/43
229	BOOSTER PUMP HOUSE (RE-USED AS STORE)	T.B.	9590/41
230	SUCTION TANK BASE	.	" - "
231	FUEL COMPOUND 70'x 40'	WIRE ENCL	-
232	BUCKET CLEANSING HOUSE	T.B.	NIL
233	STAND-BY SET HOUSE - 250 K.W. / O.M.R.		1039/41
234	FIRE TRAILOR PUMP SHED (18'x 18')	A	NIL
235-236	CYCLE SHELTER	LOCAL	
171	SPORTS STORE (45'x 18')	T.B.	
172	TECHNICAL LATRINE. W.A.A.F.	"	9026/41
173	(SITE OF) R.T. TRAINER, MORSE LECTURE ROOM		NIL
174	GYM. WITH CHANCEL & CINEMA PROJECTION ROOM	T.B.	4911/42
175	EDUCATION BLOCK (84'x 24')	S	1252/44
176	A.A. DOME TRAINER 16MM		9277/42
177	TECHNICAL LATRINE R.A.F.	T.B.	9026/41
178	A.M. BOMBING TEACHER 1- COMPT	"	6301/42
179	AIRMEN'S BARRACK HUT FOR 100	PLASTERBD	12WA/LG682
180A	" " " " 56	"	" "
180B	" " " " 56	"	" "
181	" ABLUTIONS	T.B.	" "

53

LIVING SITE NO.1

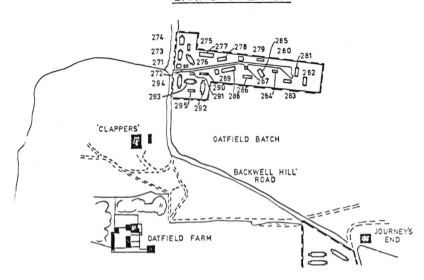

Bldg. No	Building	Constn.	Dwg. No.
271	PICKET POST WITH PROPHYLACTIC ROOM	T.B.	4830/41
272	CYCLE SHELTER	LOCAL	NIL
273	SERGEANTS QUARTERS (FOR 10) (36'x16)	N.	4931/41
274	" " " "	N.	" "
275	SERGEANTS LATRINE AND DRYING ROOM (FOR 3 HUTS)	T.B.	4830/41
276	" QUARTERS (FOR 10) (36'x16')	N.	4931/41
277	" " (B. FOR 20) (60'x19'7")	S.	3497/43
278	STATIC WATER TANK 15000 GALS.	C.	12WA/TDS 155
279	FUEL COMPOUND (15'x15')	WIRE ENCL	NIL
280	AIR RADIO SHELTER - STANTON (FOR 50)		A.M. SUPPLY
281	SERGEANTS QUARTERS (FOR 8) (36'x16')	N.	4931/41
282	" " " " "	N.	" "
283	" " " " "	N.	" "
284	" . LATRINE (FOR 3 HUTS) "	T.B.	4830/41
285	" QUARTERS(" 8) (36'x16')	N.	4931/41
286	" " (" 8)	N	" "
287	" LATRINES AND DRYING ROOM FOR 2 HUTS.	T.B.	4830/41
288	" QUARTERS (B. FOR 20) (60'x19'7")	S.	3497/43
289	" ABLUTIONS (12'x19'7")	S.	100/44
290	AIR RAID SHELTER - STANTON (FOR 50)		A.M. SUPPLY
291	TRANSFORMER PLINTH (BLAST WALLS)		NIL
292	SERGEANTS QUARTERS (FOR 8) (36'x16')	N.	4931/41
293	" " " " "	N.	" "
294	" . " " " "	N.	" "
295	" LATRINE AND DRYING ROOM (FOR 3 HUTS)	T.B.	4830/41

LIVING SITE NO.2

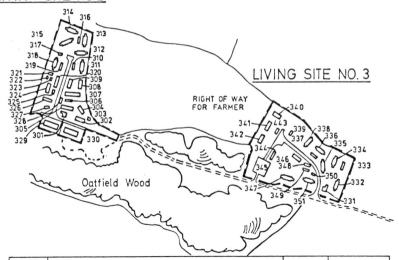

LIVING SITE NO. 3

RIGHT OF WAY
FOR FARMER

Oatfield Wood

Bldg.No.	Building	Constn.	Dwg. No.
301	PICKET POST WITH PROPHYLACTIC ROOM	T.B.	4830/41
302	OFFICER'S QTRS. AND SERVANTS WORK ROOM (FOR 3)(36'x16')	N.	4931/41
303	" LATRINE (FOR 2 HUTS)	T.B.	4830/41
304	" QTRS. AND SERVANTS WORK ROOM (FOR 3) (36'x16')	N.	4931/41
305	" (B. FOR 12) (60'x19'7")	S.	3497/43
306	AIR RAID SHELTER, STANTON. (FOR 50)		A.M. SUPPLY
307	OFFICER'S QUARTERS (B. FOR 12) (60' 19'7")	S.	3497/43
308	" (FOR 6) (36'x16')	N.	4931/41
309	STATIC WATER TANK 150,000 GALS.	C.	NIL
310	AIRMEN'S LATRINES AND DRYING ROOM (FOR 3 HUTS)	T.B.	4830/41
311	OFFICER'S QUARTERS (FOR 6) (36'x16')	N.	4931/41
312	AIRMEN'S BARRACK HUT (FOR 18) "	N.	"
313	" " " " "	N.	"
314	" " " " "	N.	"
315	" " " " "	N.	"
316	AIR RAID SHELTER - STANTON " (FOR 50)	N.	A.M. SUPPLY
317	FUEL COMPOUND (15'x15')	WIRE ENCL.	NIL
318	OFFICER'S QUARTERS (FOR 6) (36'x16')	N.	4931/41
319	" LATRINE AND DRYING ROOM (FOR 3 HUTS)	T.B.	4830/41
320	" SHOWERS (48'x19'7")	S.	9102/43
321	OFFICER'S AND AIRMEN'S ABLUTIONS (19'7"x 12')	S.	100/44
322	WATER TOWER FOR BOILER HOUSE		9102/43
323	BOILER HOUSE FOR OFFICERS AND AIRMENS ABLUTIONS	T.B.	"
324	OFFICERS QTRS AND SERVANTS WORKROOM (FOR 3)(36'x16')	N.	4931/41
325 ·	" LATRINE AND DRYING ROOM (FOR 2 HUTS)	T.B.	4830/41
326	" QTRS AND SERVANTS WORKROOM (FOR 3) (36'x16')	N.	4931/41
327	TRANSFORMER PLINTH - BLAST WALLS		NIL
328	CYCLE SHELTER	LOCAL	"
329	OFFICERS QUARTERS (B FOR 12) (60'x19'7")	S.	3497/43
330	" " " "	S.	"

LIVING SITE NO. 3

Bldg. No.	Building	Constn.	Dwg. No.
331	PICKET POST WITH PROPHYLACTIC ROOM	T.B.	4830/41
332	OFFICERS QUARTERS (FOR 6) (36'x16')	N.	4931/41
333	AIRMENS LATRINE AND DRYING ROOM (FOR 3 HUTS)	T.B.	4830/41
334	" BARRACK HUT (FOR 18) (36'x 16')	N.	4931/41
335	OFFICERS QUARTERS (FOR 6) (36'x 16')	N.	" "
336	AIRMENS BARRACK HUT (FOR 18) (36' x 16')	N.	
337	AIR RAID SHELTER-STANTON (FOR 50)		A.M. SUPPLY
338	AIRMENS BARRACK HUT (FOR 18) (36' x 16')	N.	4931/41
339	OFFICERS AND AIRMENS ABLUTIONS. (12' x 19'7")	S.	100/44
340	" QTRS AND SERVANTS WORKROOM (FOR 3)(36'x16')	N.	4931/41
341	" " " " " "	N.	"
342	" " " " " "	N.	
343	" LATRINE AND DRYING ROOM (FOR 3 HUTS)	T.B.	4830/41
344	AIR RAID SHELTER-STANTON (FOR 50)		A.M. SUPPLY
345	FUEL COMPOUND (54'x 54')	WIRE ENCL.	178 / 41
346	STATIC WATER TANK 15000 GALS.	C.	12 WA/T.D.S.155
347	OFFICERS QUARTERS (FOR 6) (36'x16')	N.	4931/41
348	CYCLE SHELTER	LOCAL	NIL
349	OFFICERS LATRINE AND DRYING ROOM (FOR 3 HUTS)	T.B.	4830/41
350	TRANSFORMER PLINTH- BLAST WALLS		NIL
351	OFFICERS QUARTERS (FOR 6) (36'x16')		4931/41

W.A.A.F. LIVING SITE

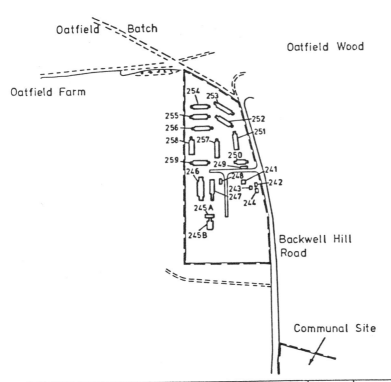

Bldg.No.	Building		Constn.	Dwg. No.
241	PICKET POST	(18'x16')	N	12404/41
242	AUTO-PNEUMATIC BOOSTING PLANT -PUMP HOUSE		T.B.	1599/44
243	" " " " PNEUMATIC TANK		S.T.	" "
244	" " " " SUCTION "		S.T.	" "
245A	OFFICERS QUARTERS (FOR 9) (36'x 18')		A	12WA/LG666
245B	" " " "		A	" "
246	W.A.A.F. LAT. LAUNDRY & HAIRDRESS'G SHOP(5 for 201/250)		T.B.	9278/42
247	" DECONTAM. BLK & BATH HOUSE (5 for 201/250)		T.B.	" "
248-249	CYCLE SHELTER		LOCAL	NIL
250	W.A.A.F. SERGEANTS QUARTERS (For 10)		A	3472/42
251	AIRWOMENS BARRACK HUT (For 30) TYPE 'B' (60'x 9'7")		S	3497/43
252	" " " " " "		S	" "
253	" " " " " "		S	" "
254	" " " " " "		S	" "
255	" " " " " "		S	" "
256	" " " " " "		S	" "
257	" " " " " "		S	" "
258	" " " " " "		S	" "
259	" " " " " "		S	" "

57

DISPERSAL SITE 1

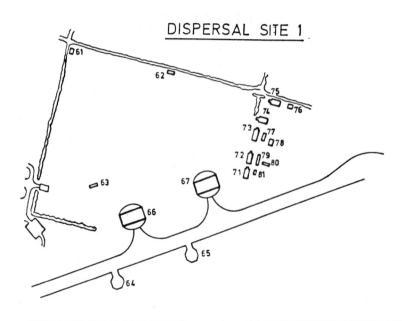

Bldg.No.	Building		Constn.	Dwg. No.
61	S.A.A. STORE	(24'x 16')	N	12725 / 41
62	GAS CHAMBER		T.B.	12411 / 41
63	P.B.X. BUILDING		BRICK	13727 / 41
64-65	HARDSTANDING		-	12 WA/TDS 358
66	HANGAR- BLISTER "E.O."		S.T.	12532 / 41
67	" " "		S.T.	"
71	DISPERSAL OFFICES	(36'x 16')	N	12 WA/ LG 571
72	CREW AND LOCKER ROOM	"	N	" "
73	MAINTENANCE ROOM AND STORE	"	N	" "
74	AIRMEN'S BARRACK HUT	"	N	4931/41
75	" " "	"	N	" "
76	TRANSFORMER PLINTH			NIL
77	AIRMEN'S LATRINES AND DRYING ROOMS	(FOR 3)	T.B.	4830/41
78	STATIC WATER TANK	(7000 GALS)	C	12 WA/TDS 155
79	CYCLE SHELTER		LOCAL	NIL
80	AIR RAID SHELTER-'STANTON' (AIR MIN.SUPPLY)			
81	SERGEANTS LATRINES AND DRYING ROOMS (FOR 1 HUT)		T.B.	4830/41

DISPERSAL SITE 2

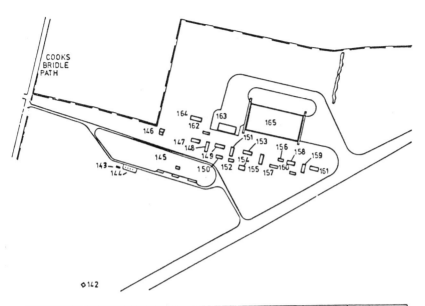

Bldg.No.	Building	Constn.	Dwg. No.
142	TRANSFORMER PLINTH		NIL
143	BULK OIL STORAGE TANK (1000 GALS.)		"
144	WASTE OIL STORAGE (CONC. BOWSER AND 4 NO. TANKS)		"
145	AVIATION PETROL INSTALLATION (24000 GALS.)		15425/40
146	TRANSFORMER PLINTH		NIL
147	RECREATION HUT (36'x 16')	N.	10024/41
148-149	AIRMEN'S BARRACK HUT (FOR 18)	N.	4931/41
150	" LATRINES AND DRYING ROOMS (FOR 3 HUTS)	T. B.	4630/41
151	SERVICING SQUADRON OFFICE (36'x 16')	N.	12 WA/ LG 627
152	CYCLE SHELTER	LOCAL	NIL
153	SERVICING SQUADRON GROUND CREW ROOM (36'x16')	N.	12WA/LG627
154	STATIC WATER TANK (7000 GALS.)	C.	12WA / LG 155
155	SERVICING SQUADRON STORE (36'x16')	N.	12 WA/LG 627
156	OFFICER'S LATRINE (FOR 1 HUT)	T. B.	4630/41
157	AIR RAID SHELTER (STANTON)		A.M. SUPPLY
158	CREW AND LOCKER ROOM (36'x 16')	N.	12 WA/ LG 571
159	FLIGHT OFFICES "	N.	" " "
160	CYCLE SHELTER	LOCAL	NIL
161	MAINTENANCE CREW AND STORE ROOM (36'x16')	N	12WA/LG571
162	TECHNICAL LATRINE (W.A.A.F.)	T. B.	9026/41
163	MAIN WORKSHOPS (72'x35')	R.	12WA/LG584
164	LUBRICANTS AND INFLAMMABLES STORE (48'x19'7")	S.	9105/43
165	HANGAR - BELLMAN :	S.T.	8349/37

DISPERSAL SITE 3

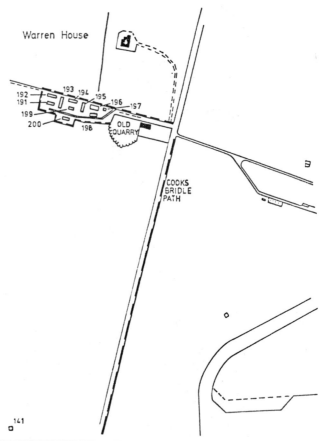

Warren House

Bldg. No.	Building	Constn.	Dwg. No.
141	MAIN BEACON (B.A.SYSTEM)		M & E 9700/41
191	AIR RAID SHELTER. (FOR 50)	C.	A.M. SUPPLY
192	RECREATION HUT (36'x 16')	N.	10024/41
193	AIRMEN'S BARRACK HUT (FOR 18) (36'x 16')	N.	4931/41
194	" " " " "	N.	" "
195	" " " " "	N.	" "
196	SERGEANT'S QUARTERS (FOR 8) "	N.	" "
197	" LATRINE AND DRYING ROOM (FOR 1 HUT)	T.B.	4830/41
198	CYCLE SHELTER	LOCAL	NIL
199	AIRMEN'S LATRINES AND DRYING ROOM (FOR 3 HUTS)	T.B.	4830/41
200	STATIC WATER TANK 7000 GALS.	G.	12 WA/T.D.S.155

DISPERSAL SITE 4

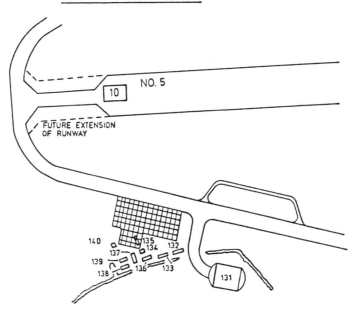

Bldg. No.	Building		Constn.	Dwg. No.
131	HANGAR - BLISTER	(DOUBLE E-O)	ST.	12532/41
132	AIR RAID SHELTER	(FOR 50)	C	A.M. SUPPLY
133	AIRMEN'S LATRINE & DRYING ROOM	(FOR 3 HUTS)	T.B.	4830/41
134	STATIC WATER TANK	(7000 GALS)	C.	NIL
135	CYCLE SHELTER		LOCAL	
136	CREW AND LOCKER ROOM	(36'x 16')	N.	12 WA/ LG 571
137	DISPERSAL OFFICES	"	N.	" "
138	RECREATION HUT	"	N.	4931/41
139	MAINTENANCE ROOM AND STORE	"	N.	12 WA/ LG 571
140	TRANSFORMER PLINTH			NIL

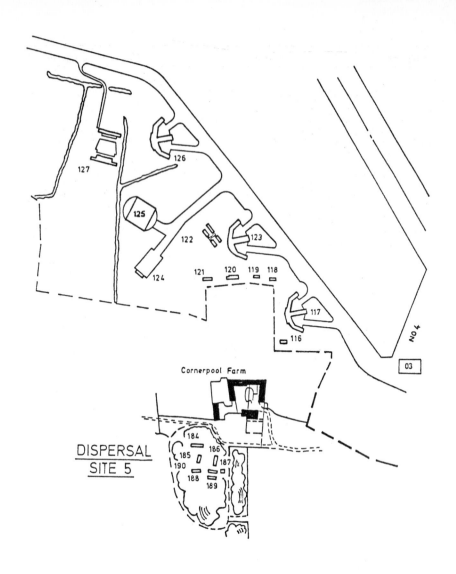

126

127

125

122

123

121 120 119 118

124

117

116

NO 4

03

Cornerpool Farm

DISPERSAL
SITE 5

184

185 186

190 187

188

189

62

Bldg. No	Building	Constn.	Dwg. No.
116	S.A.A. STORE TYPE 'B' (24'x16')	N	12725/41
117	AIRCRAFT PEN		7151/41
118	TRANSFORMER PLINTH (BLAST WALLS)		NIL
119	DISPERSAL LATRINE	T.B.	9026/41
120	SLEEPING SHELTER (FOR 33)	BRICK	11049/41
121	DRYING ROOM (16'N)	N	13214/41
122	FLIGHT OFFICE "	N	" "
123	AIRCRAFT PEN		7151/41
124	CANNON TEST BUTT	BRICK	16461/41
125	HANGAR - BLISTER (DOUBLE E-O)	ST	12532/41
126	AIRCRAFT PEN		7151/41
127	M.G. AND CANNON RANGE (4 POINT 25 YDS)	BRICK	147/41

DISPERSAL SITE 5

Bldg. No	Building	Constn.	Dwg. No.
184	AIR RAID SHELTER - STANTON		A.M. SUPPLY
185	AIRMEN'S LATRINES AND DRYING ROOM (FOR 3 HUTS)	T.B.	4830/41
186	" BARRACK HUT (FOR 18) (36'x16')	N	4931/41
187	STATIC WATER TANK 7000 GALS.	C	12WA/TDS155
188	AIRMEN'S BARRACK HUT (FOR 18) (36'x16')	N	4931/41
189	RECREATION HUT (36'x16')	N	10024/41
190	AIRMEN'S BARRACK HUT (FOR 18) (36'x16')	N	4931/41

SEWAGE WORKS SITE

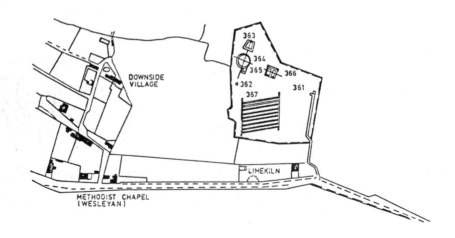

Bldg. No.	Building	Constn.	Dwg. No.
361	DESTRUCTOR HOUSE	T.B.	9559/40
362	TOOL HOUSE	"	7493/40
363	SEDIMENTATION TANK		1452/41
364	PERCOLATING FILTER		1453/41
365	HUMUS TANK		1455/41
366	SLUDGE DRYING BEDS		" "
367	SURFACE IRRIGATION TRENCHES		11179/41

MISCELLANEOUS

Bldg. No.	Building	Constn.	Dwg. No.
371	SICK QTRS. - COMBINED R.A.F. & W.A.A.F. REQUISITIONED	EXIST. BLD & S.	12 WA/LG 643
372	H.F. TRANSMITTING STATION (SITED ON LOCATION PLAN)	T.B.	625/42 • 3115/43
373	H.F./D.F. STATION (12'x12') (" " " ")		
374	REST HUT FOR H.F./D.F. STATION (21' x 19' 7")	S.	2408/43
375	BEACON - SITE 'A'		12 WA/LG 427
376	" " 'B'		12 WA/LG 428
377	" " 'C'		12 WA/LG 429